creative
photoshop®
landscape
techniques

creative photoshop® landscape techniques

Les Meehan

LARK BOOKS

A Division of Sterling Publishing Co., Inc.
New York

Creative Photoshop Landscape Techniques

10 9 8 7 6 5 4 3 2 1
First Edition

Library of Congress Cataloging-in-Publication Data

Meehan, Les.
  Creative Photoshop landscape techniques / Les Meehan.-- 1st ed.
    p. cm.
  Includes index.
  ISBN-10: 1-57990-708-3 (pbk.)
  ISBN-13: 978-1-57990-708-2 (pbk.)
  1. Landscape photography--Technique. 2. Photography--Digital
techniques.
  3. Photography--Retouching--Data processing. 4. Adobe
Photoshop. I. Title.
  TR660.M44 2006
  778.9'36--dc22

                          2005030746

Published by Lark Books, a division of
Sterling Publishing Co., Inc.
387 Park Avenue South, New York, N.Y. 10016

© The Ilex Press Limited 2006

This book was conceived by ILEX,
The Old Candlemakers, West Street, Lewes, BN7 2NZ

Distributed in Canada by Sterling Publishing,
c/o Canadian Manda Group
165 Dufferin Street, Toronto, Ontario, Canada M6K 3H6

If you have questions or comments about this book, please contact:
Lark Books, 67 Broadway, Asheville, NC 28801, (828) 253-0467
www.larkbooks.com

Printed in China

ISBN 13: 978-1-57990-708-2
ISBN 10: 1-57990-708-3

For more information on this title, please visit:
www.web-linked.com/cplpus

For information about custom editions, special sales, premium
and corporate purchases, please contact Sterling Special Sales
Department at 800-805-5489 or specialsales@sterlingpub.com.

CONTENTS

INTRODUCTION

CREATING A SUNSET
Page 106

MIST AND FOG
Page 68

Landscape, in all its myriad forms, has been a fascinating subject for creative photographers for as long as photography itself has existed. Due to the flow of time, temperamental weather conditions, and seasonal transitions, the various landscape forms of the natural world present a constantly changing visual feast. However, it is exactly this ever-changing aspect of landscape that makes it such a difficult subject to master. When you combine these uncontrollable factors with the restriction of having to record everything that the camera lens "sees" from a particular viewpoint—unlike painters who can select and re-arrange only the aspects of a scene they want to portray—it becomes clear why landscape photography can be both a joy but also a frustrating creative nightmare.

Now, with digital cameras producing high image quality and, more importantly, the accessibility of advanced image editing software such as Adobe Photoshop, many of the frustrations of traditional landscape photography have been reduced or removed entirely.

Digital imaging now gives the landscape photographer all the creative options previously only available to painters. You no longer need to be frustrated by unsuitable weather conditions, out of season colors, or undesirable features in a scene, since all of these things can now be corrected or enhanced in your digital darkroom.

To ease you into the fascinating world of Photoshop landscape photography, this book contains detailed projects ranging from simple color and contrast enhancements to generating unique weather effects. More advanced projects deal with simulating landscape features that can be placed in your scenes, creating waterfalls, and making realistic night or galactic skies for more ethereal landscape effects.

LENS FLARE
Page 164

CHANGING SUMMER TO FALL
Page 114

USEFUL BASICS

BASIC CORRECTIONS

Most pictures, unless perfectly exposed in the camera, benefit from some tonal and/or color enhancement before considering other creative options. There are several methods available in Photoshop for correcting the exposure of light or dark pictures or for removing unwanted color casts. The simplest method of adjusting the tonal range of a picture is to use a Levels adjustment layer. However, by far the most powerful method, although it is a little more complicated, is to use a Curves adjustment layer. Curves adjustment allows you to use your mouse to shape a tone curve graph to achieve very subtle corrections on specific parts of the tone scale.

Color balance problems are easily corrected using a Color Balance adjustment layer. By adjusting the sliders for the various colors in either the shadows, mid-tones, or highlights, fine color control is possible. The examples here show the basic procedures.

1 To correct pictures like this easily, create a *Levels* adjustment layer above the main image. In the *Levels* dialog move the black and white sliders below the horizontal graph axis until they are just inside the ends of the graph, as shown in the screengrab. The picture now has a more normal tonal range.

This mountain scene shows considerable haze due to the altitude and summer heat. The result is an image with lower than normal contrast and soft detail. These problems are compounded by slight overexposure.

2 As this picture shows, the altitude and heat haze over the mountain areas produce a blue color cast. To correct this type of color cast, create a *Color Balance* adjustment layer and move the sliders as needed to bring back the natural color.

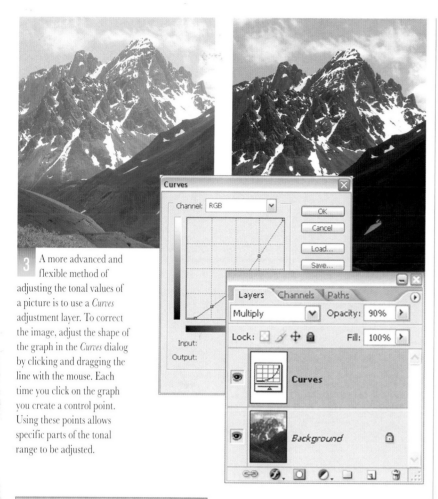

3 A more advanced and flexible method of adjusting the tonal values of a picture is to use a *Curves* adjustment layer. To correct the image, adjust the shape of the graph in the *Curves* dialog by clicking and dragging the line with the mouse. Each time you click on the graph you create a control point. Using these points allows specific parts of the tonal range to be adjusted.

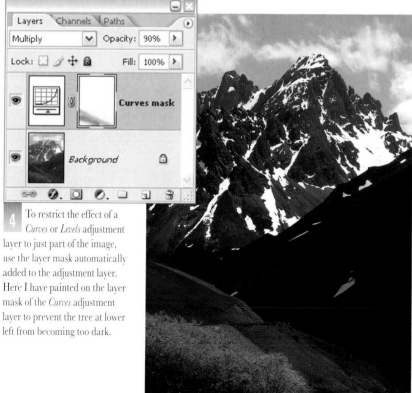

4 To restrict the effect of a *Curves* or *Levels* adjustment layer to just part of the image, use the layer mask automatically added to the adjustment layer. Here I have painted on the layer mask of the *Curves* adjustment layer to prevent the tree at lower left from becoming too dark.

5 *Curves* or *Levels* adjustment layers can also be used to correct dark pictures. In this high-contrast scene I exposed for the rocks, so the shadows recorded were too dark. Correct dark pictures using a *Curves* adjustment layer as shown here. To stop the sky becoming too light, use the layer mask to prevent the adjustment affecting the sky.

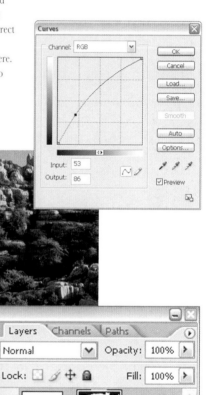

IMPROVING BRIGHT PICTURES

Histogram

Channel: RGB

Source: Entire Image
Mean: 168.28	Level:
Std Dev: 43.23	Count:
Median: 174	Percentile:
Pixels: 237000	Cache Level: 3

1 As this scene shows, bright, flat lighting combined with a predominance of middle-to-light tones results in an image that appears excessively bright. You can see this graphically by opening the *Histogram* window and examining the image graph. The histogram shows the numerical distribution of the various image tones between the extremes of black and white. Here we can clearly see that this image has few middle-to-dark tones but that the lightest tones do not exceed white.

Overly bright pictures can be caused by excessive exposure, bright or flat lighting, or an absence of darker tones (the latter are known as high-key images). These types of picture can be improved with the simple technique shown here, using the layers and blending mode facilities of the Layers palette. The main thing to look out for in bright pictures is "white-out" in the lightest parts of the image. White-out areas are too overexposed to contain any detail and cannot be recovered, even with the method shown here.

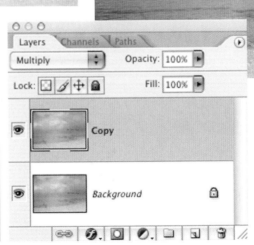

Layers   Channels   Paths

Multiply   Opacity: 100%

Lock: Fill: 100%

Copy

Background

2 Make a copy of the background layer by dragging its thumbnail in the *Layers* palette to the *Create a new layer* button at the bottom of the palette. In the *Layers* palette's *Blending mode* drop-down list select the *Multiply* option. This will darken all the tones in the image by effectively doubling their previous values.

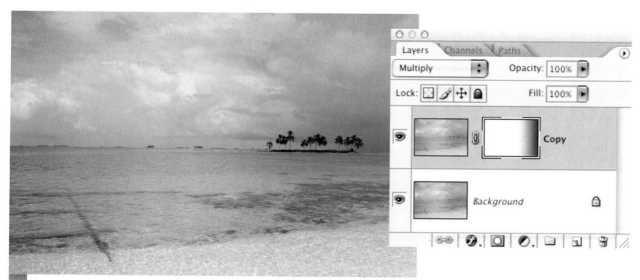

3 Sometimes, as in this picture, the natural daylight varies quite a lot from one side of the scene to the other, and the difference in tonal values becomes over-accentuated. Here, the right side of the scene is a little too dark. To correct this problem, add a layer mask to the new "Copy" layer. Choose the *Gradient* tool from the toolbox and with a black to white linear gradient drag in from the right edge almost to the center of the image. This gradient mask will prevent some of the tonal values of the "Copy" layer from interacting with those of the background layer.

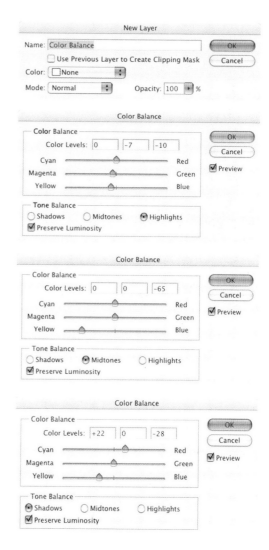

4 This image also has a rather strong blue color bias which looks unnatural, even for a tropical paradise. We can reduce this color cast by creating a *Color Balance* adjustment layer above the other layers. The settings I used for each part of the tonal range in this picture are shown in the dialog boxes. The result is a more natural, cool green color for the water in the foreground.

IMPROVING DULL PICTURES

1 This picture was taken as a large rain cloud obscured the sky, resulting in dull light. The contrast of the sky and field need to be adjusted separately to produce a more dramatic scene.

The basic techniques for correcting exposure and color that were explained in the previous pages can also be used to solve other image problems. In this example, the picture is suffering from dull lighting, which has resulted in poor contrast and reduced color saturation. The elements of the picture require a little more intensity to make the simplicity of the whole image really work. For best results, the enhancement required for the sky and ground areas are different, so we will use masked adjustment layers to facilitate these individual changes.

2 Start by making a selection of the sky using the *Magic Wand* tool. Any areas in the sky not selected the first time can be added to the selection by drawing round them with the *Lasso* tool while holding down the Shift key.

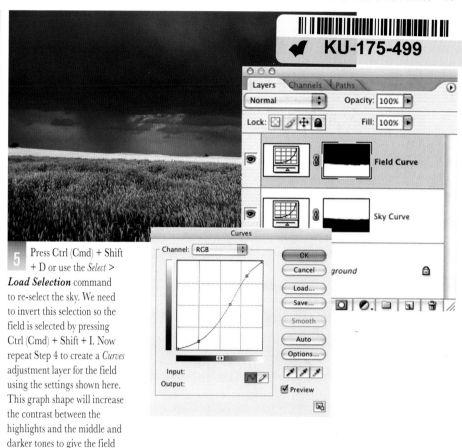

Feather Selection

Feather Radius: 1 pixels

OK
Cancel

Save Selection

Destination
Document: Dull.tif
Channel: *New*
Name: Sky

OK
Cancel

Operation
◉ New Channel
○ Add to Channel
○ Subtract from Channel
○ Intersect with Channel

3 Press Ctrl (Cmd) + Alt (Opt) + D to open the *Feather Selection* dialog and set the *Feather Radius* to one pixel. This slight feathering of the selection will help to blend the different changes to the sky and field. We will need this selection more than once, so save it to a new

Alpha channel using the *Select > Save Selection* command. In the *Save Selection* dialog, name the new channel "Sky," and in the *Operations* section make sure the *New channel* option is active.

5 Press Ctrl (Cmd) + Shift + D or use the *Select > Load Selection* command to re-select the sky. We need to invert this selection so the field is selected by pressing Ctrl (Cmd) + Shift + I. Now repeat Step 4 to create a *Curves* adjustment layer for the field using the settings shown here. This graph shape will increase the contrast between the highlights and the middle and darker tones to give the field more sparkle, and will also improve the color saturation.

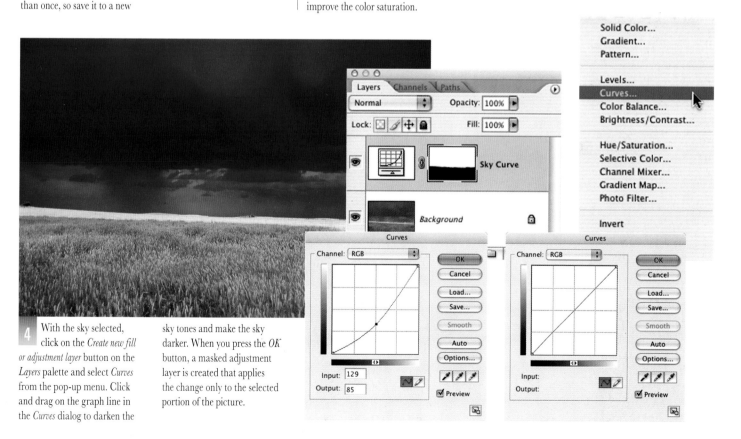

4 With the sky selected, click on the *Create new fill or adjustment layer* button on the *Layers* palette and select *Curves* from the pop-up menu. Click and drag on the graph line in the *Curves* dialog to darken the

sky tones and make the sky darker. When you press the *OK* button, a masked adjustment layer is created that applies the change only to the selected portion of the picture.

IMPROVING CITY PICTURES

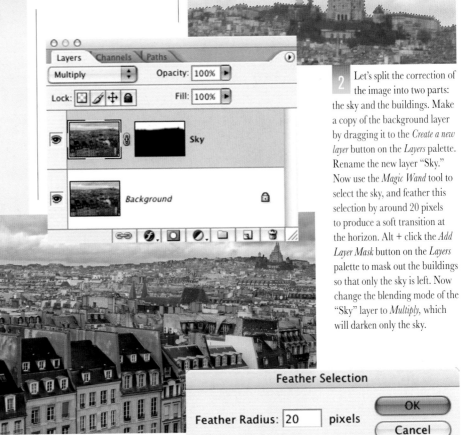

Urban landscapes and cityscapes, such as this view across the rooftops, often look more interesting in reality than in a two-dimensional picture. This kind of view requires the magic ingredient of hard, late-afternoon sunlight to bring out the various shapes that lend the scene its interest. All too often though, due to poor weather and city smog, we are faced with a scene that is rather lifeless. In this situation, the Photoshop techniques shown here can rescue the image.

1 This is a typical view across the rooftops of Paris, taken from the window of a tall building on a cloudy day. The result is flat and low in contrast.

2 Let's split the correction of the image into two parts: the sky and the buildings. Make a copy of the background layer by dragging it to the *Create a new layer* button on the *Layers* palette. Rename the new layer "Sky." Now use the *Magic Wand* tool to select the sky, and feather this selection by around 20 pixels to produce a soft transition at the horizon. Alt + click the *Add Layer Mask* button on the *Layers* palette to mask out the buildings so that only the sky is left. Now change the blending mode of the "Sky" layer to *Multiply*, which will darken only the sky.

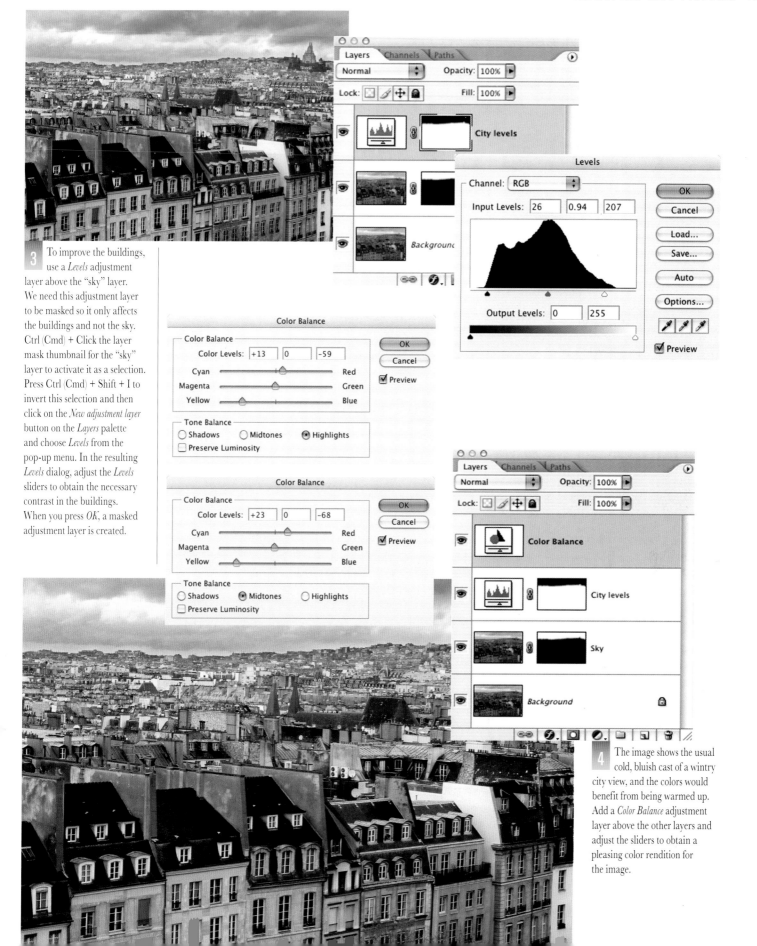

3 To improve the buildings, use a *Levels* adjustment layer above the "sky" layer. We need this adjustment layer to be masked so it only affects the buildings and not the sky. Ctrl (Cmd) + Click the layer mask thumbnail for the "sky" layer to activate it as a selection. Press Ctrl (Cmd) + Shift + I to invert this selection and then click on the *New adjustment layer* button on the *Layers* palette and choose *Levels* from the pop-up menu. In the resulting *Levels* dialog, adjust the *Levels* sliders to obtain the necessary contrast in the buildings. When you press *OK*, a masked adjustment layer is created.

4 The image shows the usual cold, bluish cast of a wintry city view, and the colors would benefit from being warmed up. Add a *Color Balance* adjustment layer above the other layers and adjust the sliders to obtain a pleasing color rendition for the image.

IMPROVING WOODLAND PICTURES

1 Spring is a wonderfully vivid season, when trees and plants show their true beauty by giving dazzling displays of color. Unfortunately, when photographed, these colors can often look dull and disappointing due to the ambient color of the light. This is one such image—note how the colors are muted rather than vibrant.

Woodland or forest scenes provide plenty of variety throughout the year for taking pictures. They adopt different colors and personalities depending on their season, enabling you to revisit the same location several times to capture the various rhythms of nature. Of course there will be many occasions, as every landscape photographer knows, when you visit a scene only to be disappointed by the prevailing conditions. It is at these times that Photoshop provides the necessary tools to bring an image back into line with your original intentions for the scene.

2 This type of image can be corrected very easily using a copy of the image on a new layer. Drag the background layer to the *Create a new layer* button on the *Layers* palette. Change the blending mode of the new layer to *Overlay* and, as if by magic, the scene is instantly transformed with more contrast and improved color saturation.

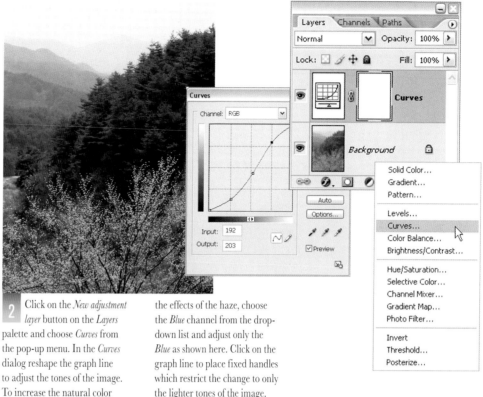

1. When the view of a woodland scene extends into the distance, as shown here, atmospheric haze reduces detail, color, and contrast towards the horizon. We can correct the latter two of these problems using a *Curves* adjustment layer.

2. Click on the *New adjustment layer* button on the *Layers* palette and choose *Curves* from the pop-up menu. In the *Curves* dialog reshape the graph line to adjust the tones of the image. To increase the natural color of the distant hills and reduce the effects of the haze, choose the *Blue* channel from the drop-down list and adjust only the *Blue* as shown here. Click on the graph line to place fixed handles which restrict the change to only the lighter tones of the image.

3. The *Curves* adjustment has removed the subtle tones from the sky, but we can recover these by masking the sky area on the adjustment mask. Click on the mask thumbnail of the *Curves* adjustment layer to activate it and use a soft-edged black brush to paint over the sky area to restore it.

4. The yellow foliage in the foreground would benefit from a little more saturation to make it more prominent in the composition. To do this add a *Hue/Saturation* adjustment layer above the background layer and move the *Saturation* slider to the right to increase the color. To restrict the saturation increase only to the foreground tree, activate the *Hue/Saturation* layer mask and paint over the rest of the image areas with a black brush.

IMPROVING WATERSCAPES

New Layer

Name: Original

☐ Use Previous Layer to Create Clipping Mask

Color: ☐ None

Mode: Normal   Opacity: 100 ▸ %

OK

Cancel

Pictures consisting mainly of large bodies of water often disappoint. This is usually due to the fact that the reflection of the sky in the water's surface results in either a flat, overly bright surface or one with a significant color cast. The problem is made worse when the sky is overcast, since there is not even any sunlight to give the existing water texture a little sparkle. Pictures of this sort need drastic, but simple, enhancement to convert them into something more interesting, and the example here shows exactly how this is done.

1 This sea and island image shows the type of result you can expect when the light is flat and dull, the sky is overcast and the sea is quite calm, creating only a slight surface texture. A strong blue color cast is also typical of such scenes. To save this image we need to improve the sea, replace the sky and bring some color back into the island's foliage.

2 The first step is to replace the dull sky with a more pleasing blue one. Double-click on the background layer thumbnail to convert it to a normal layer, and name it "Original." We need to hide the sky using a layer mask attached to the image layer. Usually, we make a selection of the sky first and then Alt (Opt) + Click on the *Add layer mask* button on the *Layers* palette. However, in this scene the horizon line is not well defined, so semi-automatic tools such as the *Magic Wand* will not be very successful. Therefore, use the *Lasso* tool to make a rough selection of the sky with the baseline just above the distant hills, and then Alt (Opt) + Click the *Add Layer Mask* button. Fine-tune the layer mask using a small, soft, black brush to paint along the line of the hills.

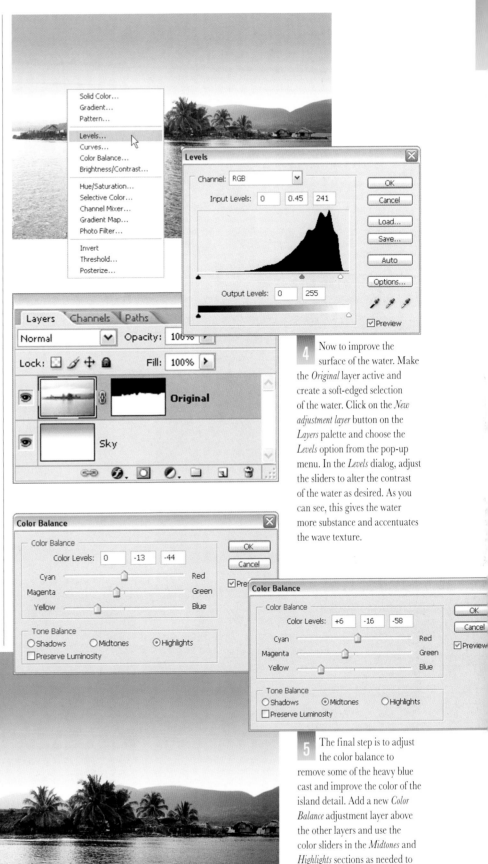

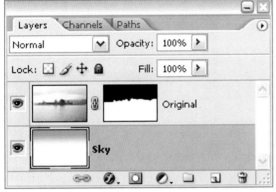

4 Now to improve the surface of the water. Make the *Original* layer active and create a soft-edged selection of the water. Click on the *New adjustment layer* button on the *Layers* palette and choose the *Levels* option from the pop-up menu. In the *Levels* dialog, adjust the sliders to alter the contrast of the water as desired. As you can see, this gives the water more substance and accentuates the wave texture.

5 The final step is to adjust the color balance to remove some of the heavy blue cast and improve the color of the island detail. Add a new *Color Balance* adjustment layer above the other layers and use the color sliders in the *Midtones* and *Highlights* sections as needed to produce a better rendition.

3 Next, Ctrl (Cmd) + Click the *Create a new layer* button on the *Layers* palette to create a new blank layer below the original layer, then rename this layer "Sky." Use the *Swatches* palette to select a pleasing sky blue (I chose *Light Cyan*) as the foreground color and make the *Gradient* tool active. Choose the *Foreground to Background* linear gradient in the *Options* bar and drag from just below the top of the image to just above the horizon line to produce a hazy, tropical sky effect.

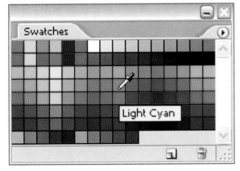

IMPROVING GRASS PICTURES

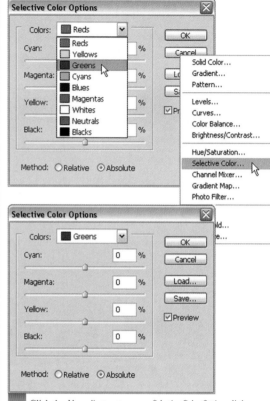

Scenes containing a limited color range, such as green fields or close-up views of grasses, can be improved by using Photoshop's color enhancement facilities. Often with such pictures you will only want to adjust the main subject, without disturbing the tones and colors in the rest of the scene. In pictures with grass as the dominant feature, as shown here, the original green color seen by your eyes is often recorded with an unpleasant cyan or blue color cast. This is due to the surface of the grass blades reflecting the color of the sky. In this picture you can clearly see this blue reflection on the surface of the water. Fortunately, this is very easy to fix.

1 The main problem here is the coolness of the color in the grasses. The prevailing conditions have left the grasses with an ugly cyan cast. Correcting this will make the green of the grasses more vibrant.

2 Click the *New adjustment layer* button on the *Layers* palette and choose the *Selective Color* command from the pop-up menu. This command allows you to adjust the individual color components of a specific color in the image. In the *Selective Color Options* dialog, open the *Colors* drop-down list and choose *Greens*. This will enable you to adjust the color components of the grasses in isolation from the rest of the scene.

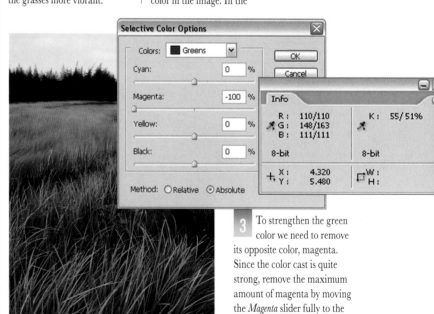

3 To strengthen the green color we need to remove its opposite color, magenta. Since the color cast is quite strong, remove the maximum amount of magenta by moving the *Magenta* slider fully to the left. You can ensure that only the green is being altered by checking the *Info* palette.

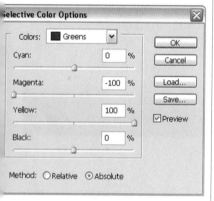

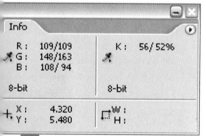

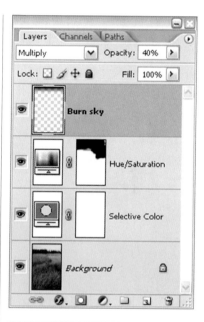

4 Close inspection shows that the grass still looks too cool, so we also need to increase the *Yellow* component to remove some of the blue cast. Re-open the *Selective Color Options* dialog by double-clicking on the adjustment layer thumbnail in the *Layers* palette. Move the *Yellow* slider all the way to the right to increase the amount of yellow—in fact, this reduces the opposite color, blue.

5 Although the green of the grass is now more vibrant and natural we can enhance it further by increasing the saturation of the image. Add a *Hue/Saturation* adjustment layer above the other layers and move the *Saturation* slider to the right, stopping at 30%. This increases the saturation of the entire image, but we want to restrict the change to the grass areas. To correct this, click on the *Hue/Saturation* layer mask thumbnail to activate it and use a soft black brush to paint over the water, distant trees, and sky areas.

6 As a final touch, reduce the excessively bright sky and focus attention on the foreground by applying a graduated filter. (See pages 26–27 for more on this).

GRAD FILTER VARIATIONS

In "Improving Waterscapes" we used a relatively standard graduated effect to improve the sky in the picture. However, there are graduated camera filters available that provide more than a simple darkening effect. Colored grad filters allow you to tint and darken the sky at the same time. Filters known as "sunset grads" have different strength color gradation on each half, allowing the top and bottom of the image to be darkened and tinted by different amounts. These and other camera grad filter effects are easy to recreate with Photoshop.

However, merely simulating the effect of camera filters doesn't utilize the enormous potential of digital methods. The examples shown here demonstrate just a few of the possibilities, some of which are only feasible using digital techniques.

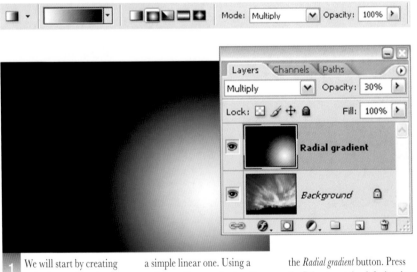

1 We will start by creating a simple, graduated darkening effect similar to that used in "Improving Waterscapes." However, the unique aspect of this variation is that we use a radial gradient to create the effect, rather than a simple linear one. Using a radial gradient emphasizes the wide-angle distortion effect of the lens. Create a new layer in *Multiply* blending mode. Select the *Gradient* tool. In the *Options* bar choose the *Foreground to Background* gradient and click the *Radial gradient* button. Press the D key to set the default colors and then the X key to reverse them. On the new layer drag the mouse from near where the sun has set to the top of the picture, just left of center, to produce the graduated effect.

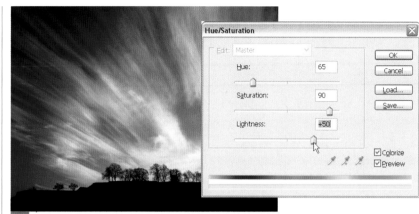

2 The radial gradient darkened all the tones covered by the gradient, which reduced the values of the clouds as well as the sky. To retain the brightness of the clouds we can use the *Select* > **Color Range** command to make a selection of only the blue color in the sky. Since the blue gets stronger from the horizon outwards, the *Color Range* command creates a graduated selection which can then act like a graduated filter.

4 We can take the color range version one step further by adding color to the filled layer. With the new layer active, use the *Hue/Saturation* command with the *Colorize* option checked to alter the color of the sky. The settings you choose will dramatically change the appearance of the picture.

5 Colored grad filters are used to add color to, as well as darken, the sky. The most popular color used is known as "tobacco" and produces results similar to those shown here. To create any color grad effect, simply create a new layer in *Multiply* mode and apply a Linear gradient from the top of the picture to just above the horizon line. Make the Foreground color whatever color you desire for the effect. Here I have chosen the Light Red Orange from the *Swatches* palette as the foreground color. Note that the color is applied to all covered areas, resulting in some clouds having color while others do not.

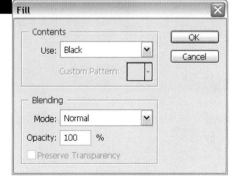

3 With the selection active, create a new layer and press Shift + F5 to open the *Fill* dialog. Choose *Black* from the *Use:* drop-down list and press *OK*. Change the blending mode of the layer to *Multiply* and, if necessary, adjust the *Opacity*. Note how the clouds have retained their sparkle in this version.

Tip

A sunset grad filter can be simulated in Photoshop in a similar way to a standard colored grad, except you need to reduce the density of the gradient from the bottom of the image as well as the top. On a new layer in *Multiply* mode, create the sky gradient and select the warm color as before. Set the *Gradient Tool* options bar to *Multiply* mode and the *Opacity to 50%*. Then add a second gradient from the bottom of the image.

DODGING AND BURNING

Traditional darkroom printing relies heavily on the art of local dodging and burning in order to either lighten (dodge) or darken (burn) specific areas of a print. This allows for considerable creative expression during exposure. Although Adobe Photoshop has features dedicated to this task, called the "Dodge" and "Burn" tools, these work on the actual image pixels and so only on a specified part of the tonal range.

A more elegant and controllable method is to use a layer filled with 50% gray above the main image. Set this layer to "Overlay" blending mode and paint on it using the normal brushes and the default colors of black or white. By adjusting the opacity setting of the brush you can dodge or burn any part of the image as desired. Since the layer is in "Overlay" blending mode, any tone darker than 50% gray will darken the image, while any tone lighter than 50% gray will lighten the image. Also, if you make a mistake or change your mind later, simply paint over the area with 50% gray to restore it. This method makes it very easy to create complex burning and dodging effects on any image.

1 An image like this requires quite a lot of local dodging and burning to change the visual emphasis of the composition. Use the *Layer > New Layer* command to create a new layer, and name it "Dodge and burn." In the *New Layer* dialog, change the mode to *Overlay* and click in the check-box to automatically fill the layer with 50% gray.

Tip
When using this method of dodging and burning with soft brushes on a layer, drawing accuracy is not essential to obtain good results.

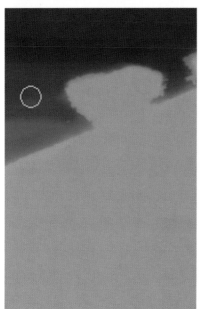

2 Select the default colors by pressing D on the keyboard and choose a soft brush to paint with. To burn in (darken) choose *Black* as the *Foreground* color and reduce the *Opacity* on the *Options* bar. The higher the opacity, the greater the effect, so start with a low opacity setting (you can always go over the same area more than once). In this scene I have darkened the pale hillside in the far distance. The effect on the "Dodge and Burn" layer is shown in the screengrab.

3 Continue in the same way to produce more complex dodging and burning. As can be seen in this final image, the composition is more balanced as a result. Compare this to the original image and examine the "Dodge and Burn" layer to see the various densities used.

COMPLEX SELECTIONS

It is important for anyone using digital imaging software to master the process of making selections and to become familiar with the various selection tools and methods on offer. A simple selection is often the first step towards the creation of a more complex mask for use in controlling how an image is affected by subsequent changes. It is essential to choose the correct tool and method when making a new selection as it can save time and effort later.

Digital landscape images often present problems when it comes to creating selections. It may be necessary to isolate the sky from the ground, and this is complicated by objects such as trees and foliage when they cover part of the sky. Also, the distant horizon in many landscape images is often quite soft due to atmospheric haze and reduced depth of field. The selection tools that are normally used on subjects with simple outlines and well-defined edges are inappropriate for complex shapes and soft horizons.

Here we will examine three ways to make a complicated selection. The first two utilize two of Photoshop's standard tools—the Magic Wand and the Color Range command. The third method uses the Color Channels palette and the Levels command to produce an otherwise difficult mask. No one method is necessarily the best; it depends entirely on what is being selected in a particular image.

1 This simple but effective picture contains the classic selection problem: intricate foliage silhouetted against the sky. In addition, the sky requires darkening in order to add greater impact and bring out the subtle clouds.

Tolerance: 32 ☑ Anti-alias ☑ Contiguous ☐ Sample All Layers

2 The *Magic Wand* tool is one of the most used selection methods in Photoshop. It is a very versatile tool and can produce complex selections quickly. Unfortunately, in the image shown here, the many areas where the sky is surrounded by fronds makes using the *Magic Wand* tool rather tedious. However, the solid tower in the picture is an ideal candidate for this tool. One important aspect of the *Magic Wand* tool is its *Tolerance* setting on the *Options* bar. When the tool is clicked in the image, the tolerance value determines how much variation from the first tone will be selected. The higher the value, the wider the range of tones and colors selected. Adjust this value when selecting soft-edged subjects in order to achieve the best result. Also, use the Shift and Alt (Opt) keys when clicking with the tool to add or subtract from the existing selection. The screengrab shows the tool being used to select around the tower.

3 Another useful selection method is to select specific colors in an image. This can be especially effective in landscape images, where the sky is often a totally different color to the land areas. Specific colors can be selected using the *Color Range* command on the *Select* menu.

This method proved ideal for the image shown here since it allowed all the various tones of the blue sky to be selected without including other areas.

The *Color Range* dialog enables you to sample various areas of the image to include in the selection using the plus and minus eyedroppers. The selected areas are shown in the preview window. The *Fuzziness* value is similar to the *Tolerance* value of the *Magic Wand* tool. The resulting selection mask and its effect on the sky can be seen in the illustrations. It is often helpful to apply a little *Gaussian* *Blur* to the mask to help blend any edges. Once the selection is created, it can be saved for future use in an *Alpha* channel using *Select* > **Save Selection**.

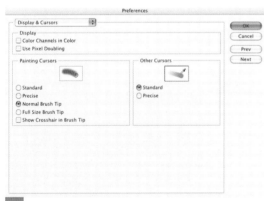

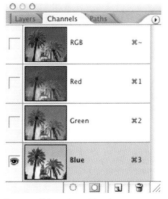

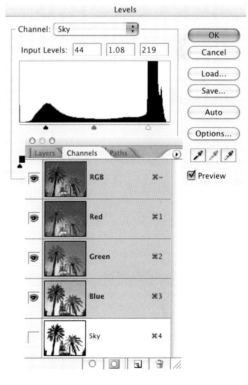

4 You can also use the color channels of the image to create complex selections and masks. Start by making sure that the *Color Channels in Color* option is not selected in the *Display and Cursors* preferences. Then activate the *Color Channels* palette and find the channel with the best contrast around the area to be selected. Then copy this channel to a new channel to form a mask. This new mask channel can be further adjusted using the *Levels* command and the painting tools to form any mask you need.

In this example, checking the *Color Channels* palette shows that the *Blue* channel has the best contrast between the sky and foliage. Copy the channel by dragging it to the *Create new channel* button at the bottom of the palette. Use the *Levels* command to increase the contrast as needed, but be careful not to allow all those little gaps in the leaves where the sky shows through to become blocked. It is interesting to compare the final mask with that produced by the *Color Range* command. Note that this method did not include all of the tower.

CREATING ROCKS

Rocks are a fundamental part of many landscape pictures and are often central to their overall composition. Many of the greatest landscape photographers have realized the visual significance of a dominant rock in the foreground. Traditionally, we have been at nature's mercy when trying to find just the right kind of rock in exactly the right place.

Now, with Adobe Photoshop at our command, relying on chance is a thing of the past. In this project we will look at one way of creating realistic digital rocks that can be inserted into landscape scenes.

1 The first step is to create a new file at a useful size and resolution. For this project start with a file 6 inches (15cm) square at 300 dpi. Next, create a new layer named "Rock" using the *Layer > New Layer* command.

2 We need to create a random pattern, but first the pattern's colors must be set. Press the D key to set the default colors and then click on a dark gray color in the Swatches palette to set the foreground color. Click the *Set background color* box on the toolbox and choose a medium brown from the *Color Picker* dialog.

3 To create the pattern, make sure the "Rock" layer is active and apply the *Filter > Render > Clouds* filter. To give the resulting pattern a little "grit," apply the *Noise > Add Noise* filter with a low *Amount* setting and both the *Gaussian* and *Monochrome* options checked.

Tip
It is a good idea to save different basic rock shapes without any three-dimensional shading in a Rock library folder. You can apply specific shading and color as required when using the individual rocks in a composition.

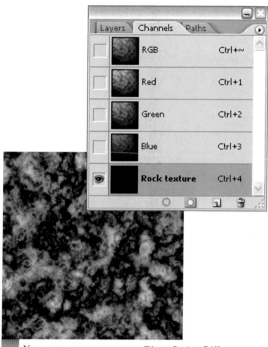

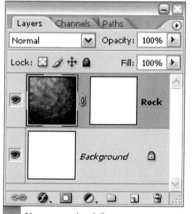

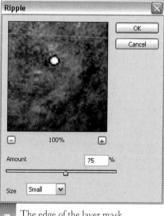

4 Now to create a texture channel for use later with the *Lighting Effects* filter. Open the *Channels* palette and make a new channel by clicking the *Create new channel* button. Name this channel "Rock texture." With this channel active, apply

Filter > Render> Difference Clouds. Add some noise with the *Noise > Add Noise* filter. Finally, apply the *Difference Clouds* filter a few more times to make the design more random.

6 Next, we need to define the shape of our rock. Choose an interesting area of the pattern and use the *Lasso* tool to draw the shape of your desired rock as a selection. With the selection active, add a layer mask to the rock texture layer using the *Reveal Selection* option.

7 The edge of the layer mask is quite smooth so we need to roughen it a little. Make sure the "Rock texture" layer mask is active and apply the *Distort > Ripple* filter. We now have a rock, although it is a little flat-looking.

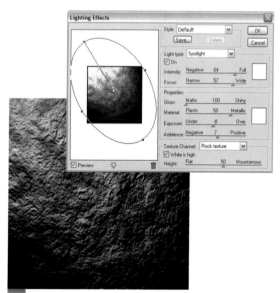

5 To create the actual texture for the rock, use the *Lighting Effects* filter. Make the "Rock" layer active and open the *Filter > Render > Lighting Effects* dialog. Use settings similar to those shown in the screengrab. In the *Texture*

Channel drop-down list, be sure to select the "Rock texture" and move the *Height* slider to 100 (this value will determine the three-dimensional effect of the rock surface). The result should be a fairly realistic rock texture.

8 The final step is to add some shading to the rock to simulate a more three-dimensional shape. Create a new layer above the rock layer and set it to *Overlay* mode. Now choose a low-opacity brush of black or white and paint shadows and highlights over the rock to represent natural light and shade.

High Contrast

1 For the first camera exposure of a high-contrast scene such as this, calculate the exposure to retain the necessary details in the land area only. The sky will inevitably record too bright.

One of the problems facing landscape photographers is dealing with the contrast range of a scene, or the difference between the darkest and lightest of a scene's main areas. This range is measured with a light meter and is known as the Subject Brightness Range, or SBR. The unique SBR of a scene depends on several factors: the tonal values inherent in the scene, the lighting conditions, and the photographer's interpretation. Unfortunately, it is often the case that the SBR may not match the DDR (Digital Density Range, or number of stops that can be recorded in one exposure) of your digital camera, resulting in less than perfect images.

When the SBR is more or less than the DDR it is necessary to shoot two (or more) different exposures to obtain the result you want. The exposures should be carefully chosen to record the important parts of the SBR exactly as you want them. To determine the two exposures required, calculate the first exposure based on the lightest parts of the scene you wish to record, and the second on the darkest. This will ensure you extract all the desired detail from the scene.

2 The second exposure should be based on the bright sky, in this case to retain the subtle cloud on the left. Since the sun is directly to the left, and a wide-angle lens is being used, the sky tone varies in brightness across the picture.

This can be adjusted later.
Open the two image files in Photoshop and copy the darkest image into a new layer above the background layer of the lighter image, as shown in the screengrab above.

3 Now each image is on a separate layer, use the selection tools (I used the *Magic Wand*) to select the sky area of the top layer. Make the selection as accurate as possible. With the selection active, choose the *Add Layer Mask > Reveal Selection* command to mask out everything but the selected sky.

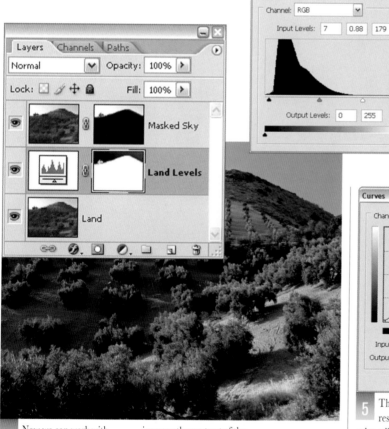

4 Now we can work with the various adjustment layers to enhance the tones and colors in separate parts of the image. Here we see the result of applying a *Levels* adjustment layer above lowest layer to increase the contrast of the olive trees and improve the mood of the scene. The values used are shown in the screengrabs. Use the layer mask of the adjustment layer to selectively apply the changes.

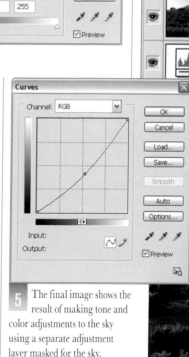

5 The final image shows the result of making tone and color adjustments to the sky using a separate adjustment layer masked for the sky. Although this method can be quite demanding, it offers the most flexibility when adjusting the separate parts of the image.

CREATING REALISTIC SHADOWS

1 Although Photoshop has a layer style for creating drop shadows, which is useful for some situations, it is more useful to know how to create a shadow from scratch.

To make a basic shadow, create a selection around the element that needs the shadow and press Ctrl (Cmd) + J to copy the element to a new layer.

There will be occasions when one of your landscape pictures doesn't contain the desired shadows. This will usually be due to the weather at the time the image was created. Generally, the more overcast the sky, the less apparent the shadows will be, so this may need to be remedied later in Photoshop. Another situation where needing to know how to create realistic digital shadows is useful is when producing a montage of both real and digitally created elements.

Before you can create realistic shadows it is necessary to understand what causes different types of shadows. This project will not only show you how to create various types of shadow, but also tell you why they need to be different to be realistic. I have used a digitally created background image and one of the digital rocks from the previous project for maximum clarity.

2 Next, add a new blank layer below the isolated element layer and press Shift + Ctrl (Cmd) + D to reactivate the previous selection. On the new layer, fill the selection with black. Press Ctrl (Cmd) + D to deselect the shadow.

3 The first thing to appreciate about shadows is their direction. This is entirely dependent on the light source in the scene. If the shadow is pointing away from you, the light source must be somewhere in front of the subject.

Conversely, if the shadow is pointing toward you, the light source is somewhere behind the subject. For a front-lit subject our basic shadow is now ready to have its shape and angle adjusted. For a back-lit subject we first need to apply the *Edit*

> *Transform* > **Flip Vertical** command to flip the shape over, then use the *Move* tool to drag the shadow downward so it is seen below the original element. Stop when the shadow is touching the extreme edge of the element.

4 To create the intended direction of light with our basic shadow we use the *Transform* > **Distort** tool to adjust the shape and simulate perspective, as shown above. It is important to consider how the shadow relates to the scene and other elements to obtain the correct perspective and to integrate the visual effect.

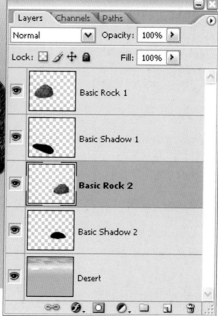

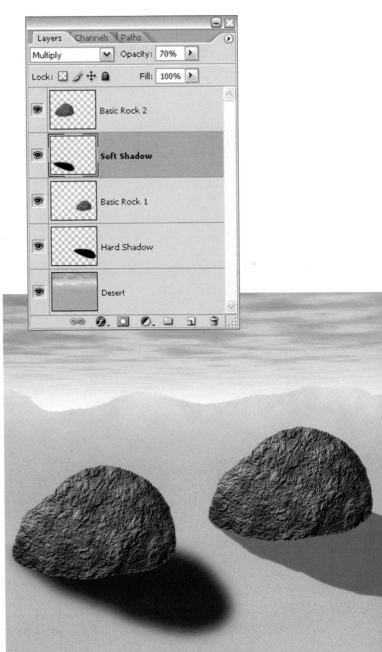

5 The next important aspect of the shadow to consider is the quality of the light. This determines how the shadow's edge will look. If the light is very hard, as in direct sunshine, the edge of the shadow will be sharp. When light becomes more diffuse and softer, for example if the sun moves behind a cloud, the edge of the shadow changes to become progressively softer and less distinct. In completely overcast weather it may not be possible to see a shadow at all. To simulate this aspect of light quality, use the *Gaussian Blur* filter to soften the edge of the shadow. Here we see the result of using a small and a large amount of blur.

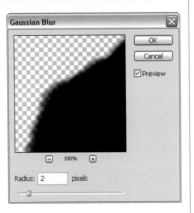

6 Once the shadow shape and edge definition have been established to simulate the light direction and quality, it is time to consider the shadow's depth of tone. How light or dark a shadow appears is determined by the amount of reflected light from the environment entering the shadow. In sunny weather with plenty of white clouds in the sky, there is lots of reflected light entering the shadows, so they are brighter than when there is only sunshine. Objects near the shadow will also reflect light back into the shadow to lighten it further. In this way, it is normal for shadows in a scene to vary in tone depending on their relationship to other objects. We control the shadow tone by changing the shadow layer's blending mode to *Multiply* and then adjusting the *Opacity* setting to obtain the desired tone. Here, the left shadow has an opacity of 70% and the right shadow 40%. Note the different mood established by each tone.

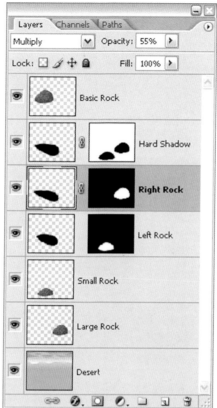

8 The final step is to integrate the elements to create a cohesive whole. Start by varying the opacities of the partial shadows on the smaller rocks to simulate the difference in reflected light on each rock. Then add some sand along the bottom edges of the rocks to bed them into the environment.

7 The final aspect of the shadow is how it interacts with other objects in the scene. A shadow will follow the contours of the surface or surfaces upon which it falls. In this way the shape of the shadow can become distorted, as its shape changes when the contours change. Compare the two versions of the rock group shown here. In the top group, the shadow has not been modified to take account of the contours of the other two rocks over which it falls. In the other, copies of the shadow on new layers have been reshaped with the *Transform > **Distort*** tool and unwanted parts hidden using layer masks formed from the rocks over which the shadow travels.

MONTAGE

1 Montage is best approached with a reasonably good idea of what you want to achieve, so the first step is to assemble the various pictures to be used. The concept for this project is "The Gateway to Hades." We will use three different pictures, shot in similar conditions, to create it.

Photomontage is almost as old as photography itself and was an essential darkroom skill for landscape photographers due to the limitations of the early light-sensitive emulsions. In those days the only way to have a good sky in a picture was to overprint a scene with a separate sky negative.

Throughout the history of photography, photomontage has been employed by artists to produce images that were simply not possible by any other means. Montage is an important technique which allows photographers to produce images that make diverse statements, from political satire to grand tableaux. Montage is also a vital tool used daily in the movie industry when special effects are needed.

Since digital montage is now available to anyone using Photoshop, without the need for specialist photography skills, it is easy to let your imagination and creativity roam free to produce whatever image you desire. The project shown here demonstrates many of the essential, but simple, techniques that can be used to create a non-existent landscape.

2 Start by opening the separate image files, and then drag each element onto the main background image. This will create a new layer for each. Name each layer appropriately.

Layers / Channels / Paths

Normal | Opacity: 100%

Lock: | Fill: 100%

Statue

Arch

Bridge

3 If necessary, use the *Clone Stamp* tool to remove unwanted details from each element. Here the buildings are being removed from the top of the ridge.

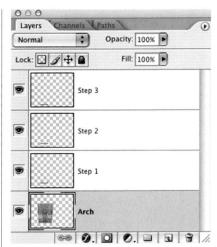

4 If the elements have been shot from different angles it will be necessary to correct any perspective imbalance. Here I am using the *Transform > Distort* command from the *Edit* menu to correct the convergence in the arched door surround. To make this easier, press Ctrl (Cmd) + R to show the rulers and drag some vertical and horizontal guides from the rulers onto the image.

5 If you need to replicate parts of an element—I wanted more steps below the door—make a selection around the area and press Ctrl (Cmd) + J to copy it to a new layer. Use the *Transform* tools to edit the new layer. Here, the step on each layer is enlarged slightly using the *Transform > Scale* command and dragged into position while the scale handles are still visible. When the steps are complete, link each step layer with the arched door and merge into one layer by pressing Ctrl (Cmd) + E.

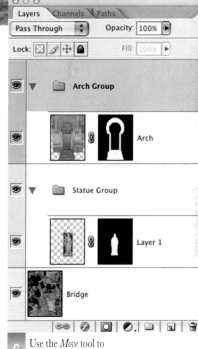

6 Use the *Move* tool to roughly position each element on its layer and order the layers so the elements will overlap as needed. Since montages usually require many layers, it is a good idea to create layer sets, as shown here, for each element. Add a layer mask to each element layer and use the various selection tools to mask out unwanted parts of the element.

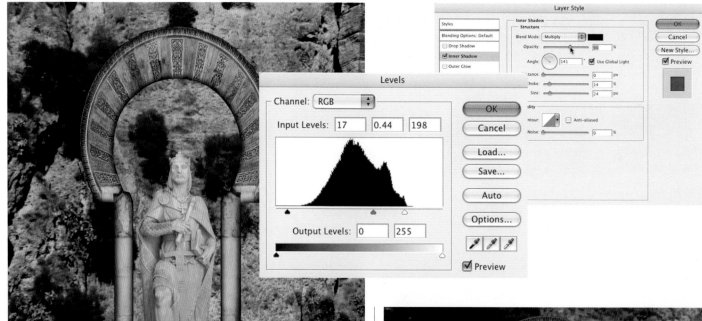

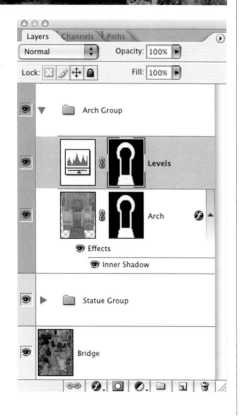

7 Next, use masked adjustment layers: Ctrl (Cmd) + Click on the element layer mask to activate it as a selection, and alter the contrast and color of each element so it balances with the background. Elements with flat lighting, like this arched door, can be made more three-dimensional by adding an *Inner Shadow* layer style to the element. Only flatten these layers when you are sure nothing more will need to be done.

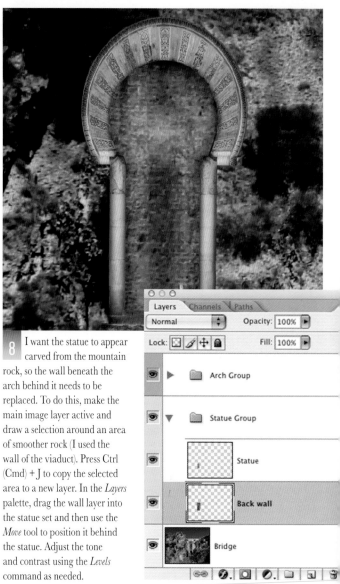

8 I want the statue to appear carved from the mountain rock, so the wall beneath the arch behind it needs to be replaced. To do this, make the main image layer active and draw a selection around an area of smoother rock (I used the wall of the viaduct). Press Ctrl (Cmd) + J to copy the selected area to a new layer. In the *Layers* palette, drag the wall layer into the statue set and then use the *Move* tool to position it behind the statue. Adjust the tone and contrast using the *Levels* command as needed.

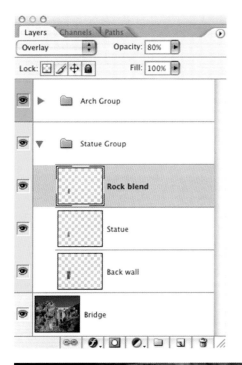

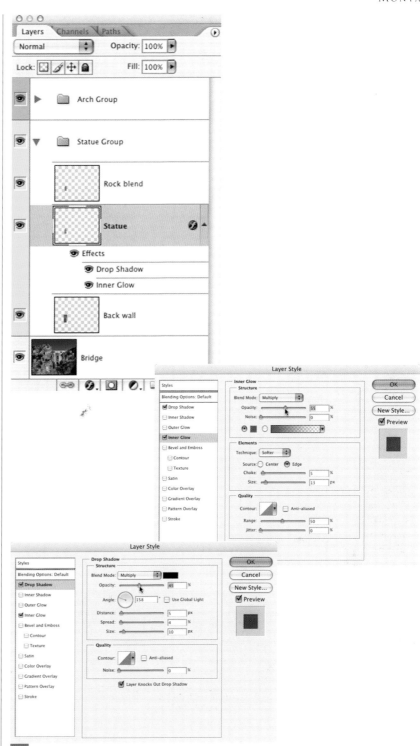

9 Now the arch element is finished we can complete the statue of the knight. Since the figure is meant to be carved from the rockface, we need to match its texture to its background by using a section of rock. Ctrl (Cmd) + Click on the statue layer to activate it as a selection. Then, with the selection tool active, drag the selection over an area of rock. Press Ctrl (Cmd) + J to copy this area to a new layer and drag the layer into the statue set above the statue layer. Change the blending mode to *Overlay* and reduce the *Opacity* setting to around 60%. This applies some of the rock detail to the statue.

10 To make the statue more three-dimensional apply an *Inner Glow* layer style to the statue using a dark gray color and the other settings shown. To give the impression of soft, directional light, also apply a *Drop Shadow* layer style. Adjust the settings to produce the desired effect.

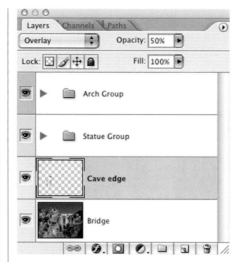

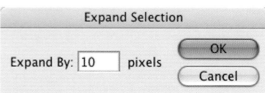

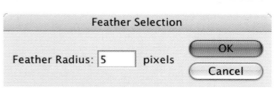

11 To make each of your elements fit into a scene you may need to adjust their sizes using the *Transform > **Scale*** command. It is your choice as to when you do this, but here I wanted the arched door and statue to be almost complete before scaling to size. To scale both the arch and statue together, so their relative sizes remain the same, link their layer sets. The scale transform will then be applied to both equally.

12 To make an element work in the context of the surrounding scene, it may be necessary to create some shadow or other impression of the element on the background. Here the archway should look set into the rockface, so some of the rock around the outer edge of the arch needs darkening. Using an expanded and mildly feathered selection of the archway to restrict the shading effect, choose a black brush and paint on a new layer above the main scene. Change the layer to *Multiply* mode and reduce its *Opacity* setting as desired.

Tip
Unless you want your montage to look unnatural,
ensure that all the individual elements you want to
include have been photographed in a similar light.
If the shadows within each element are not similar
in quality and tone, the differences will be very
apparent in the final montage.

13 To increase the visual effect of one object being part of another, it is useful to have some of the background overlap the new object. In this picture, the foliage on the rockface is ideal to overlap onto the arch. To achieve this, add a layer mask to the Arch set and paint out the arch where you want the foliage to overlap. To increase the realism of the arch the set layer mask can also be used to create a little weathering on the arch edges, simulating corrosion and gradual ruin.

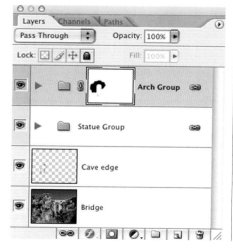

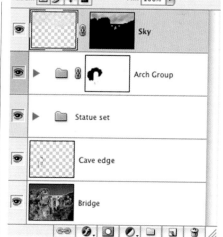

14 The final step is to add an interesting sky, created here using the *Render > Clouds* filter and a layer mask. This method is explained in detail in the "Stormy Sky" tutorial on pages 54–59.

REFLECTIONS

1 This village plaza image contains buildings whose façades are at different angles to the camera, so it is not possible to simply create a mirror image of the scene as a reflection. Each of the buildings' perspective planes will need to be handled individually to produce a collection of realistic reflections.

Reflections are found in objects that are wet or have a naturally shiny surface. Many natural subjects only become reflective when wet. For example, dry paving stones are transformed into a reflective surface after rain, and this can positively transform an urban or village scene. Creating a reflection of natural objects, such as a sky reflected in the surface of a lake, is very easy since there are usually few perspective problems. However, when creating reflections of buildings the natural perspective caused by the viewpoint of the picture can create difficulties. Two- and three-point perspective, which is commonly seen in pictures of buildings, requires careful manipulation of the reflected image.

It is very useful to be able to simulate reflections of buildings with perspective, and this project will show you exactly how to do it.

2 Start by making a selection of the first façade on the left of the image. Use the *Rectangular Marquee* tool and drag a box around the façade, with the left side running down the corner where it joins the façade's center. Press Ctrl (Cmd) + J to copy the selection to a new layer and rename it "Left."

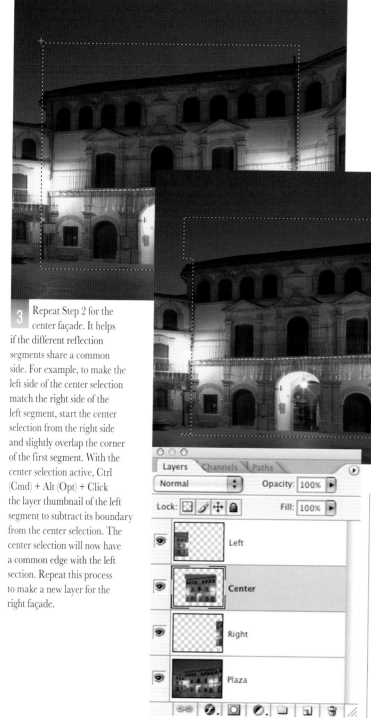

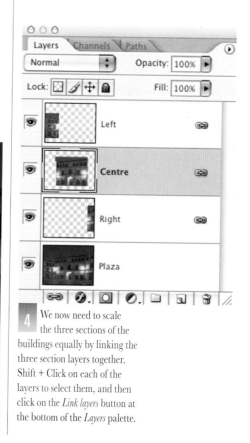

3 Repeat Step 2 for the center façade. It helps if the different reflection segments share a common side. For example, to make the left side of the center selection match the right side of the left segment, start the center selection from the right side and slightly overlap the corner of the first segment. With the center selection active, Ctrl (Cmd) + Alt (Opt) + Click the layer thumbnail of the left segment to subtract its boundary from the center selection. The center selection will now have a common edge with the left section. Repeat this process to make a new layer for the right façade.

4 We now need to scale the three sections of the buildings equally by linking the three section layers together. Shift + Click on each of the layers to select them, and then click on the *Link layers* button at the bottom of the *Layers* palette.

5 Now use the *Transform/ Scale* command on the *Edit* menu and drag the top handle downward to foreshorten the reflection images.

6 Once the images have been scaled, use the *Edit > Transform > Flip Vertical* command to make a mirror image of the buildings. Use the *Move* tool to roughly position the flipped images so the bottom of the walls almost align. Now unlink the layer by repeating the process in Step 4.

7 To correct the perspective of each segment layer, we need to use the *Transform* commands to reshape and align each section accurately with the base of the walls. Start with the Left layer and reduce the layer *Opacity* to 50%. Then use a combination of the *Distort* and *Skew* commands to adjust the shape of the section. When you're done, reset the *Opacity* to 100%. Repeat this procedure for the other two sections.

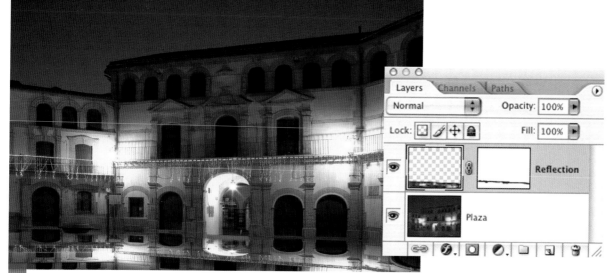

8 When the section layers are ready, link them together, merge them into one layer and rename it "Reflection." We need to blend the reflections created in Photoshop with the walls in the image, so add a layer mask to the "Reflection" layer and paint along the join line with a soft, medium-sized black brush. For this image I used a 35-pixel brush size.

9 Reduce the *Opacity* of the "Reflection" layer to reduce the mirror-like effect so that it appears more natural. The opacity of the "Reflection" layer determines the visibility of the reflection and the impression of water on the ground. The more visible the reflection, the wetter the ground seems to be. Here the *Opacity* is set at 30%.

10 The final step is to introduce some distortion to the reflection using the *Distort* > **Ocean Ripple** filter. The distortion in the reflection represents movement across the water's surface on the ground. Less distortion simulates a smoother water surface.

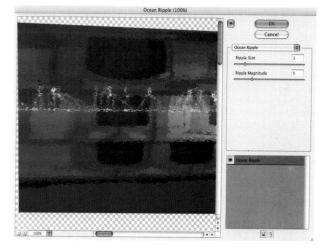

SKIES

FLUFFY CLOUDS

In landscape photography, one element that can make the difference between an average picture and a good one is the presence of clouds in the sky. The look and distribution of clouds will help determine the mood of the scene, whether the view is dark and stormy, or pastoral and tranquil.

However, as with many natural phenomena, clouds rarely behave how you want them to at the moment the photograph is taken. It is therefore very useful to be able to create your own clouds which can be inserted into otherwise unsatisfactory skies. These digital clouds can then be scaled to exactly the right size and placed in just the right position for your composition.

In this project we will generate the classic, fluffy, cumulus cloud, usually found floating majestically across a blue sky in warm summer weather.

1 Create a new file. For this project I created a file of 6" x 4" (15 x 10cm) at a resolution of 300 dpi. This will produce a cloud that can be scaled easily for either large or small pictures. To make it easier to see the cloud, fill the background layer with a sky-blue color.

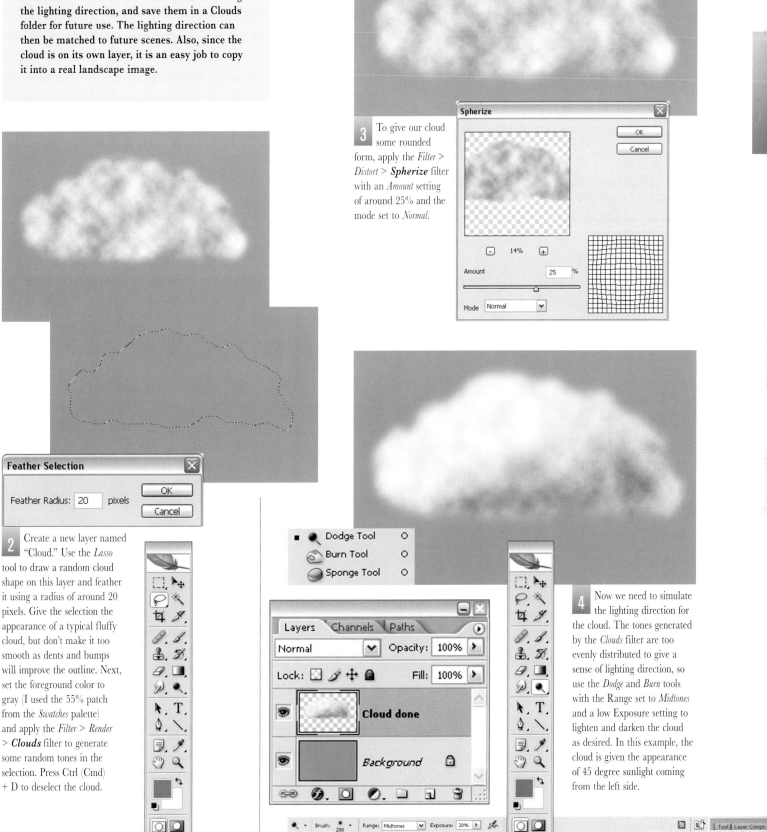

Tip

Generate several different clouds without setting the lighting direction, and save them in a Clouds folder for future use. The lighting direction can then be matched to future scenes. Also, since the cloud is on its own layer, it is an easy job to copy it into a real landscape image.

3 To give our cloud some rounded form, apply the *Filter > Distort > Spherize* filter with an *Amount* setting of around 25% and the mode set to *Normal*.

Spherize

OK
Cancel

14%

Amount   25   %

Mode   Normal

Feather Selection

Feather Radius: 20 pixels

OK
Cancel

2 Create a new layer named "Cloud." Use the *Lasso* tool to draw a random cloud shape on this layer and feather it using a radius of around 20 pixels. Give the selection the appearance of a typical fluffy cloud, but don't make it too smooth as dents and bumps will improve the outline. Next, set the foreground color to gray (I used the 55% patch from the *Swatches* palette) and apply the *Filter > Render > Clouds* filter to generate some random tones in the selection. Press Ctrl (Cmd) + D to deselect the cloud.

Dodge Tool
Burn Tool
Sponge Tool

Layers   Channels   Paths

Normal   Opacity: 100%

Lock: 🔲 ✏ ✚ 🔒   Fill: 100%

Cloud done

Background

4 Now we need to simulate the lighting direction for the cloud. The tones generated by the *Clouds* filter are too evenly distributed to give a sense of lighting direction, so use the *Dodge* and *Burn* tools with the Range set to *Midtones* and a low Exposure setting to lighten and darken the cloud as desired. In this example, the cloud is given the appearance of 45 degree sunlight coming from the left side.

Brush: 200   Range: Midtones   Exposure: 20%

Tool   Layer Comps

STORMY SKY

Dramatic storm clouds always add a real sense of drama and mystery to a landscape picture. Most of us have pictures of potentially interesting subjects that lack that one vital ingredient, a great sky. Using Photoshop means this is no longer a problem, as we can simply create whatever type of sky we desire for a particular subject and mood.

In this project we will create realistic, dramatic storm clouds and apply them to the type of picture that typically requires spicing up.

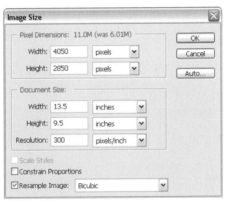

1 Start by creating a new file in which to make the storm clouds. For this project the final image is 13.5" x 9.5" (33.75 x 23.75cm), so, as shown in the dialog above, we will create a cloud file that is approximately 75% of this size.

2 If necessary, reset the default foreground and background colors by pressing D on your keyboard, and apply the *Render > Clouds* filter to fill the layer with random tones. Adjust the tones using the *Levels* command to obtain a moody range typical of storm clouds. Now use the *Image > Image Size* command to make the cloud file the same size as the main image file.

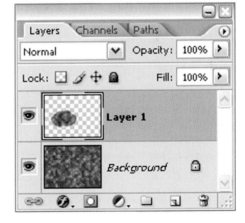

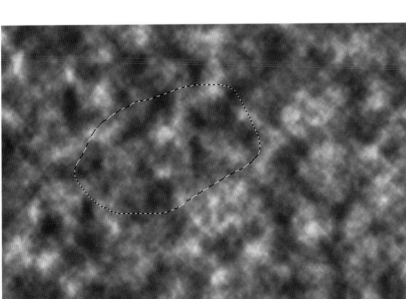

3 To give the cloud effect more depth we need to create some shape variation within the tones. Choose the *Lasso* tool, set the *Feather* option to around 50 pixels, and create a random but regular selection on the background layer. With the selection active, press Ctrl (Cmd) + J to copy the selection to a new layer. Repeat this process several times to produce various different shapes on individual layers. Remember that you will need to activate the background layer before each new selection.

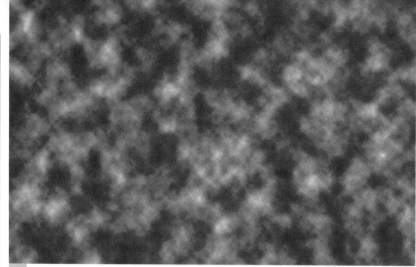

Tip

The actual size of the cloud file will affect the final size of the clouds we produce later. Smaller clouds are perceived to be at a higher altitude than larger ones, as their small size makes them seem further away. This visual effect can thus be controlled by file size; create small clouds by choosing a cloud file the same size or larger than the final image size, and create larger clouds by having the cloud file smaller than the final image size. Once ready, the cloud file can be re-sized to equal that of the final image. This method retains greater quality in the clouds and offers more control than simply scaling a clouds image layer in the final image.

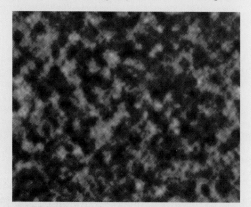

High clouds

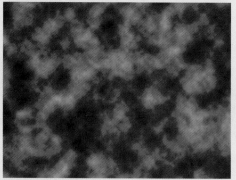

Low clouds

4 Use the *Move* tool on each layer to rearrange the various new shapes. You may also need to change the order of the layers for the best effect. Subtly adjust the tones of each shape using the *Levels* command to create a more three-dimensional effect, and use the *Eraser* tool with a soft brush to blend the edges of the shapes if necessary. When you're ready, link the layers together and merge them. Our stormy sky is now ready to use.

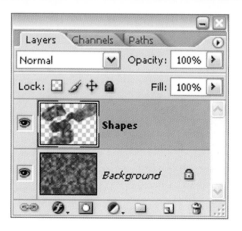

5 Open the picture you want to add the storm clouds to and make an accurate selection of the existing sky. With an image containing a clear blue sky, use the *Color* *Range* command from the *Select* menu to easily create a selection of the sky. Save the selection for use in the following steps.

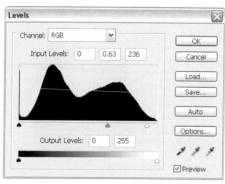

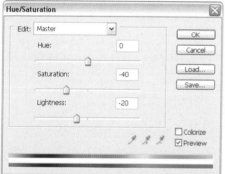

6 The sky is far too blue and bright for our stormy effect, and the contrast of the castle is too low for the feeling of dramatic light required in the picture. With the sky selection still active (if it's not, load it using the *Select > Load selection* command), add a *Hue/Saturation* adjustment layer to the image. Reduce the *Saturation* to remove some of the blue color and reduce the *Lightness* to darken the sky a little. Now use the *Select > Invert* command to invert the sky selection and add a *Levels* adjustment layer to increase the contrast of the castle.

7 Now to add the storm clouds to the main image. With the clouds image active, press Ctrl (Cmd) + A followed by Ctrl (Cmd) + C to copy the clouds to the clipboard. Return to the main image and load the sky selection by pressing Ctrl (Cmd) + Alt (Opt) + 4. Paste the clouds into this selection by pressing Ctrl (Cmd) + Shift + V. The clouds are now on a new layer and masked to show the castle. Don't worry if your clouds are the wrong size; we will adjust them in the next step.

8 Make sure the clouds thumbnail in the *Layers* palette is active by clicking on it, and use the *Edit > Transform > **Distort*** command to reshape the clouds and add some perspective as required. Make certain that the chain link icon between the layer mask and clouds thumbnail is not visible (click it to hide), or the scale transform will also scale the layer mask. Use the *Clone* tool with a soft, large brush to fill in the blank areas.

9 Now we can refine the shape of our storm clouds. With black set as the foreground color (press the D key), use a large, soft brush with an *Opacity* setting of around 30% and paint on the "Clouds" layer mask to produce areas of varying translucency. Use this method to define the edge of the cloud shapes.

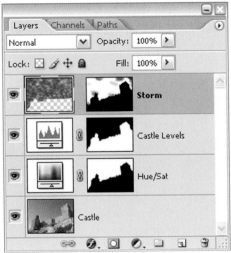

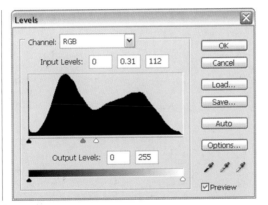

10 Since our storm clouds were created in grayscale they are unnaturally neutral in color. To rectify this, load the "Clouds" layer mask as a selection by Ctrl (Cmd) + clicking on it, and add a *Hue/Saturation* adjustment layer above the "Clouds" layer. Click the *Colorize* box in the dialog and make a subtle adjustment to the color of the clouds by selecting a yellow/brown hue and a low saturation value.

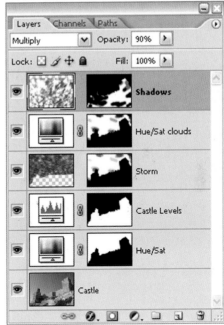

11 As a final, optional step you can add cloud shadows onto the main subject areas of the picture. Copy the "Clouds" layer to a new layer above the rest and discard the existing layer mask. Now flip the image using *Edit > Transform > **Flip Vertical***. Change the blending mode to *Multiply* and remove the light and middle tones using the *Levels* command. Add a new layer mask and paint on to it to hide unwanted shadows. Adjust the *Opacity* setting of this layer so the shadows are similar in tone to those of the original image.

COSMIC SKY

M an's exploration of space has given us an opportunity to see spectacular images of the Universe that would never otherwise have been possible. Incredible views of distant galaxies and the beautiful colors of cosmic gas clouds produce some of the most awe-inspiring space images.

Here on Earth there are similar wonders to be photographed. The Northern Lights produce spectacular displays that span the sky, but unfortunately such sights can only be seen by a lucky few.

We can create similar visual effects using Photoshop. This project will show you how to create a realistic night sky featuring a simulation of the Northern Lights.

1 Choose an image with interesting ground detail, such as the rock formations in this picture, and use adjustment layers to make any tone or color adjustments needed. Since the image will be darkened later I have lightened the shadow areas. Also, convert the background layer into a normal layer by double-clicking on it. Rename it "Land."

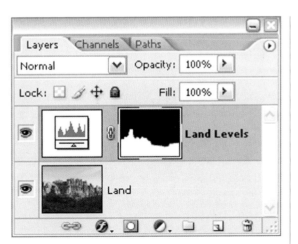

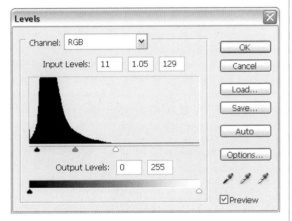

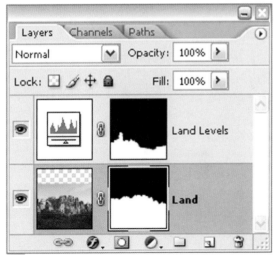

2 When the sky area is too small, as here, we need to create room for the new sky by increasing the canvas size. Use the *Image >* **Canvas Size** command to open this dialog and increase the *Height* value. Make sure to set the *Anchor* point in the dialog at bottom center.

3 Now we have space for the new sky, we need to hide the existing sky. Make a selection of the sky and save it to a new channel using the *Select >* **Save selection** command. With the sky selection still active, add a layer mask to the "Land" layer to hide the old sky.

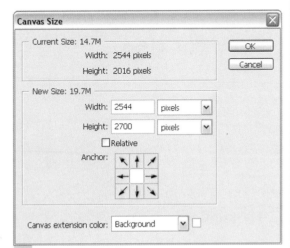

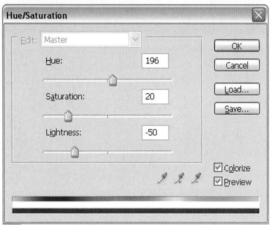

4 To create a night-time effect, add a *Hue/Saturation* adjustment layer using the values shown in the dialog. Make sure the *Colorize* box is checked. This coloring will give the image an eerie mood.

5 We want a graduated sky for the image, so first load the previously saved sky selection. Create a *Gradient fill* layer by clicking the *Create new fill* button at the bottom of the *Layers* palette. In the *Gradient* dialog, set the values shown, then click the gradient box and adjust the *Opacity* midpoint position. Click *OK* on each dialog to close it. The loaded selection will restrict the gradient to the sky area.

7. To further reduce the
stars and also increase
their size, apply a very small
amount of *Gaussian Blur* and
repeat the *Levels* adjustment.
Do this two or three times.

7. To further reduce the
stars and also increase
their size, apply a very small
amount of *Gaussian Blur* and
repeat the *Levels* adjustment.
Do this two or three times.

6. To add stars to our night
sky, create a new layer
above the rest and fill it with
black. Add some noise and
then use the *Levels* command
to increase the contrast of the
layer. This will reduce the
number of stars. Now change
the blending mode to *Screen*.
To further reduce the stars
and also increase their size,
apply a very small amount of
Gaussian Blur and repeat the
Levels adjustment. Do this two
or three times. Now remove the
stars from the rocks by loading
the sky selection and adding a
layer mask to the stars layer.

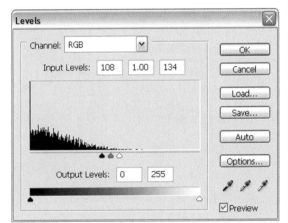

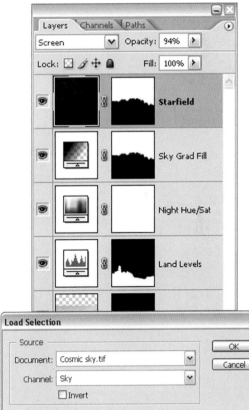

8. Now remove the stars
from the rocks by loading
the sky selection and adding a
layer mask to the stars layer.

9 The scene is now set for adding the Northern Lights effect. Create a new layer named "Lights" above the stars layer so that the stars will be behind the effect. On the "Lights" layer draw a randomly shaped selection using the *Lasso* tool and generously feather this selection. Use

Filter > Render > Clouds to fill the selection with random tones, and deselect the shape. Now apply *Filter > Render > Difference clouds* several times, adjusting the *Levels* of the shape between applications of the filter to generate unusual shapes. This is our "Northern Lights" gas cloud.

10 To make the gas cloud more interesting, use the *Liquify* filter to manipulate the shape. Use large and small brush sizes as desired and experiment until you are happy with the result. When ready, change the blending mode of the "Lights" layer to *Screen* and reduce the *Opacity* to blend it into the sky.

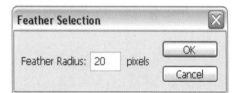

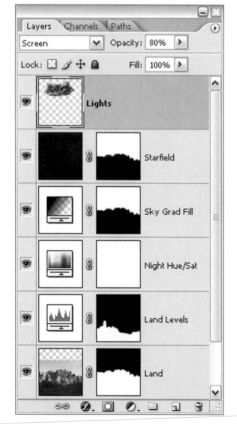

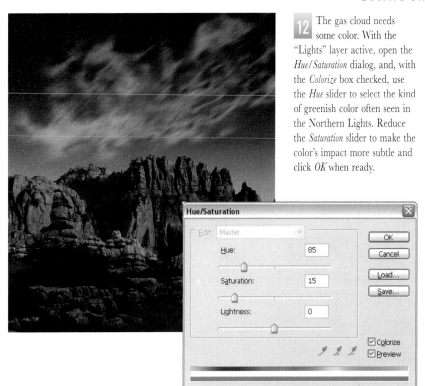

12 The gas cloud needs some color. With the "Lights" layer active, open the *Hue/Saturation* dialog, and, with the *Colorize* box checked, use the *Hue* slider to select the kind of greenish color often seen in the Northern Lights. Reduce the *Saturation* slider to make the color's impact more subtle and click *OK* when ready.

11 You can manipulate the shape of the gas cloud using the *Edit > Transform > Distort* command. Then create the impression of movement in the cloud by applying the *Filter > Blur > **Motion Blur*** filter.

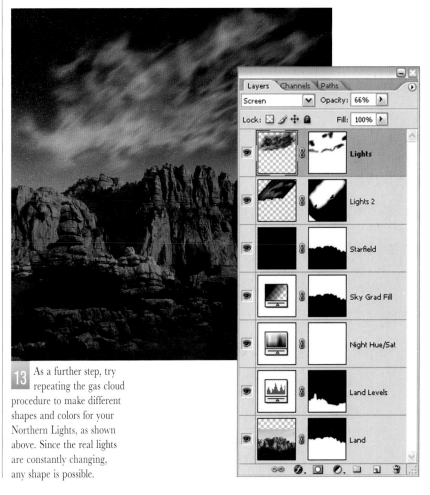

13 As a further step, try repeating the gas cloud procedure to make different shapes and colors for your Northern Lights, as shown above. Since the real lights are constantly changing, any shape is possible.

MIST AND FOG

Mist and fog result from the evaporation of moisture as the sun warms the land, and is most often seen in the early morning after rain or a heavy dew. Large bodies of water, such as lakes, also tend to produce mist when daybreak occurs due to the increase of air temperature at the surface of the water. An interesting feature of mist over water is that it often swirls and flows due to localized air currents caused by rapid temperature changes. Another important aspect of mist is that its general density is variable and it looks denser with increased distance. You will probably have experienced this effect when driving in foggy conditions.

To create the most convincing mist and fog effects, incorporate these natural features of real mist and fog into your digital reproduction.

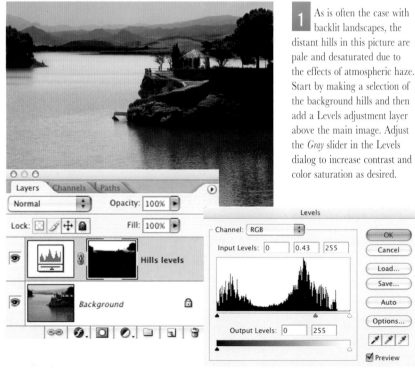

1 As is often the case with backlit landscapes, the distant hills in this picture are pale and desaturated due to the effects of atmospheric haze. Start by making a selection of the background hills and then add a Levels adjustment layer above the main image. Adjust the *Gray* slider in the Levels dialog to increase contrast and color saturation as desired.

2 Start by creating a new layer and naming it "Mist." Since I want the mist to become thinner as it spreads into the distant hills, we need to create a variable selection to control its density. First, choose the *Gradient* tool. In the *Options* bar, select the standard black to white gradient and click the *Linear gradient* button. Press Q on the keyboard to enter *Quick mask* mode and drag upward with the mouse from just below to slightly above the top edge of the lake to create a gradient. Press the Q key again to convert this gradient into a variable selection.

3 Fill the selection with variable tones by setting the Foreground color to 50% gray from the *Swatches* palette and applying the *Render > Clouds* filter.

4 We now need to introduce some perspective to the mist and scale it to fit the scene—this will also introduce a feeling of movement in the mist. With the mist layer active, use the *Transform > Perspective* command from the Edit menu and drag the top left corner handle to the left to create the desired perspective. Next, use the *Transform > Scale* command to stretch the width of the mist and lower the top edge to below the horizon line.

Twirl

OK

Cancel

100%

Angle   -20 °

ZigZag

OK

Cancel

100%

Amount   2

Ridges   2

Style   Around Center

5 The *Perspective* command always leaves empty space on two edges of the image; this space needs to be filled using the *Clone Stamp* tool. Press S on your keyboard to activate the tool and sample from the mist to fill in the gaps at the sides.

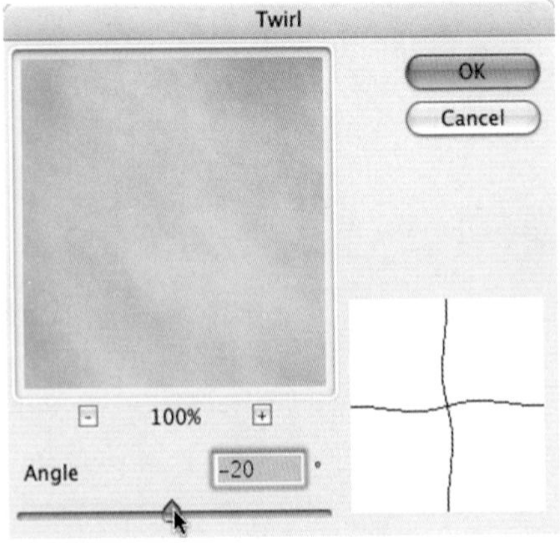

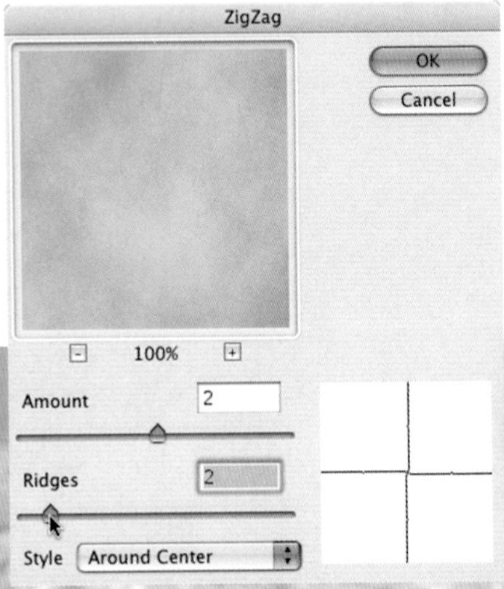

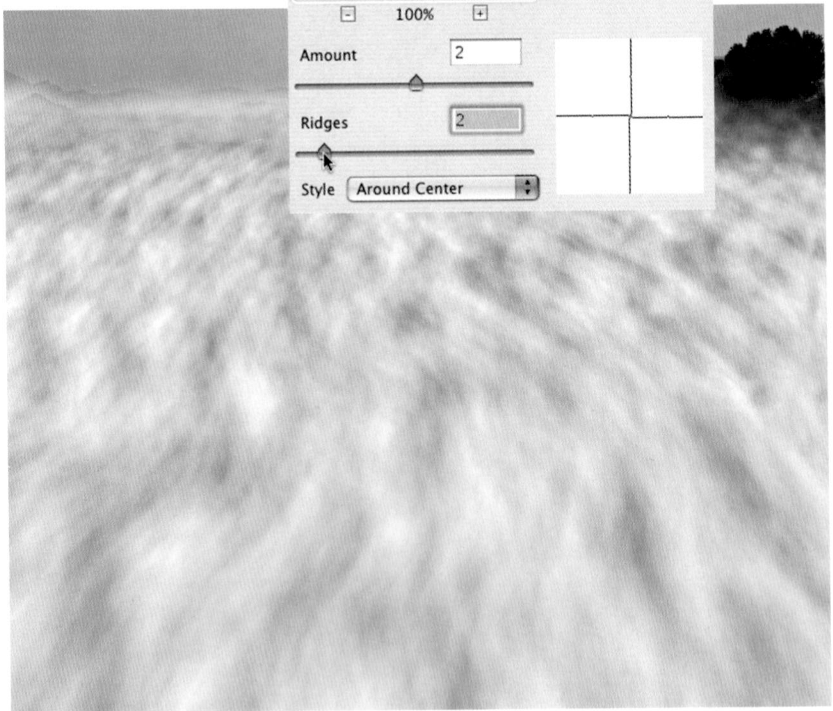

6 To add extra random movement to the mist apply the *ZigZag* filter followed by the *Twirl* filter to the mist layer. Use very small settings for the filters, as shown in the dialogs.

Tip
Mist and fog tend to glow and appear more ethereal when the light comes from behind the mist, as seen in many movies. Your digital mist will look more interesting if you start with a picture containing backlighting.

7 It is time to decide which parts of the image you want the mist to cover, and the density of local areas within the mist. Add a Layer mask to the mist layer and use different sized soft brushes with various *Opacity* settings to paint out the mist from the scene. *Opacity* settings less than 100% will reduce the density of the mist, allowing you to create a more natural, random density effect.

8 Here we see the result after completing the painting on the layer mask for the "Mist" layer. In this version the mist is quite dense, creating a very strong effect more like low fog. This can be varied to look more like a light, evaporating mist, as shown next.

9 To change the visual effect, simply adjust the overall density of the mist by reducing the mist layer *Opacity* and changing the blending mode to *Lighten*. The final step, if necessary, is to crop the image to the desired shape. Here I have removed some of the excess lake from the bottom of the image to tighten the composition, and also added some buoys in the water to create a lead-in line.

RAIN

Tip
An important consideration when simulating wet weather is the reflections seen on wet surfaces in the scene. A reflection is created when the angle of view is such that a virtual image of an object in the scene is bounced off any wet surface towards the camera lens. These reflections can be created in Photoshop using the transform tools to generate realistic mirror images of the real objects in the picture. Care is needed to match the scale and perspective of the simulated reflections to the real objects.

Although rain is one of nature's less pleasant weather conditions for a photographer, it can produce some interesting results in your pictures. Fortunately, by using digital techniques we no longer have to risk ruining expensive camera equipment in wet weather, as it is fairly easy to simulate rain effects in Photoshop.

As with all digital recreations of natural phenomena, the first thing to do is consider the natural attributes of the conditions being simulated. Rain can take many forms—from light, wispy drizzle to huge, heavy drops of water pounding the environment. Falling rain tends to reduce visibility and contrast and often changes the colors in a scene. Colors close to you look more saturated, but as distance increases, the wetness reduces saturation due to increased reflections from the wet surfaces.

1 This night-time picture was selected because it contains objects at different distances from the camera, which makes for more interesting reflections, and areas of darker tone which will help show the rain.

2 Start by creating and then saving a selection of the flat surfaces on the ground plane. As it is this plane that will be wet in the rain, this is where the reflections will be seen. Here the selection has been made in *Quick mask* mode, which is useful when generating a selection that requires both sharp outlines and areas with softer edges. Complex selections take time and are usually used extensively, so be sure to save them!

3 To create the necessary reflections for the scene, follow the steps in the Reflections project on pages 46-49. Now load the saved ground selection and use it to add a *Layer Mask* using the *Reveal Selection* option. This restricts the mirror image to the ground area only.

4 Use the same procedure to produce reflections for the foreground objects in the scene and position the reflection images in the correct place for each object. Normally, each object will require a separate layer. Use the saved selection of the ground to make a layer mask and modify it to isolate only the reflection of the object concerned. In the above image the reflections are complete except for the left side of the statue's railings.

Tip
The important visual characteristics to consider before starting to add simulated rainfall to an image are scene contrast, color saturation, reflections, and the droplet size and speed of descent of the "rain." An almost infinite range of possibilities exists with which to imbue a picture with just the right "wet" look.

Water Tones
The following process can be used to make a layer containing a random background texture. This layer can add natural variance to otherwise "perfect" images, such as the reflections in the Rain tutorial.

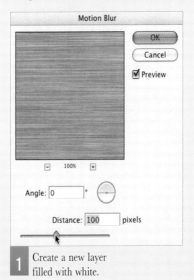

1 Create a new layer filled with white.

2 Apply Noise.

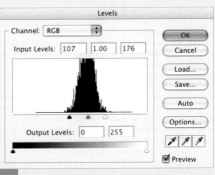

3 Apply Motion Blur (Direction set to zero).

4 Use Levels to increase contrast.

The final result as ready to apply to the picture in this project is shown here. The inverted ground selection is ready for unwanted parts of the layer to be deleted.

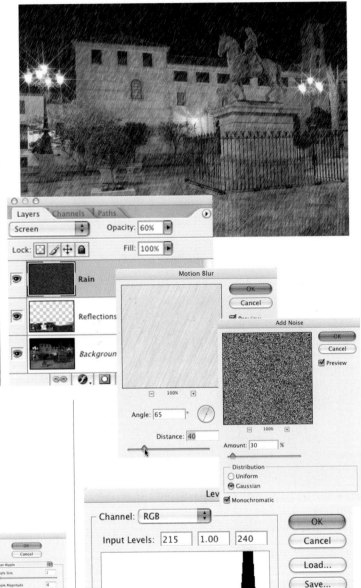

5 Once the reflections are complete, link the relevant layers and collapse them into one layer. Name this layer "Reflections" and change the blending mode to *Soft Light*. To soften the reflections, as they would look if rain was falling on the wet ground, apply a little *Gaussian Blur*. The amount of blur you choose depends on the type of rain you are simulating; the heavier the rainfall, the more blur should be applied. Reduce the *Opacity* of the reflection layer to allow some of the ground detail to show through.

To add variation to the wet floor, create a new layer filled with random tones above the reflection layer (see the "Water Tones" boxout on page 73).

Heavy rain distorts the reflections on the ground more than light rain. This distortion can be simulated by applying the *Distort > Ocean Ripple* filter to the reflections layer. Try to make the distortion proportional to the rain effect you are adding to the image.

In this picture we are creating quite a heavy looking downpour so the reflections need to be distorted a reasonable amount.

6 To make the rain effect, create a new layer named "Rain" and fill it with white. Then apply the *Noise > **Add Noise*** filter with the settings shown in the dialog. Next apply the *Blur > **Motion Blur*** filter. The Angle and Distance values will determine the type of rain effect produced. The Angle value will change the impression of the wind on the rain and the Distance value will determine the impression of light, medium, or heavy rainfall. Choose these values as required for your image. Next, use the *Levels* command to increase the contrast of the rain using the settings shown in the dialog. Finally, change the blending mode to Screen and reduce the *Opacity* to around 60%.

7 Rain is seen more clearly against darker parts of a scene, so we can use a Dodge and Burn layer to darken some surfaces in the scene. Use the *New Layer* command to create a new layer in *Overlay* mode filled with 50% gray. With the new layer active, paint over selected surfaces with a 50% black brush to darken them. Use different brush opacities to control the results. The final dodge and burn layer for this image is shown above.

8 The density of rainfall varies across a scene, and we can simulate this using a layer mask on the "Rain" layer. Also, for additional realism we can reduce the visibility of the rain against light areas of the scene. Add a layer mask to the "Rain" layer and use a large soft black brush with a low *Opacity* value, around 20%, to paint over areas where you want the rain to appear less dense. As shown here, the layer mask doesn't need to be precise and can have various opacities on it to randomize the density effect.

9 Since rain reduces color saturation with depth, add a *Hue/Saturation* adjustment layer at the top of the stack and reduce the *Saturation* to -30. Apply a black to white gradient to the *Hue/Saturation* layer mask to make the saturation reduce gradually from front to back. You may also want to paint out areas such as the statue in the foreground to restore some color. The *Layers* palette screengrab shows the final array of layers used.

WATER DROPLETS

Concentrating your visual attention on the smaller details of nature is one of the most fascinating aspects of landscape photography. Focusing on the minutiae rather than the broad vista provides many opportunities to capture often overlooked details. Generally, the most popular subjects are flowers and plants, close study of which is often rewarded with strong, graphic imagery.

Pictures of foliage often benefit from the addition of water droplets on petals and leaves. Their presence creates the impression of a recent rain shower, giving the foliage a fresher look. Here I will demonstrate a method of creating digital water droplets that can be used in a variety of situations.

1 This close-up of a leaf is an ideal candidate for water droplets. As with any new image, start by amending the contrast using a *Levels* or *Curves* adjustment layer.

3 To create the water droplets we use several layer styles working together. Create a new layer above the image and set the blending mode to *Screen*. Next, add the following layer styles: *Drop Shadow*, *Inner Glow*, and *Bevel and Emboss*, using similar settings to those shown in the screengrabs below. Once the layer styles have been added, use the *Lasso* tool to draw various shapes and sizes of water droplets onto the layer and fill these selections with black. As the selections are filled, you will see the effect of the layer styles.

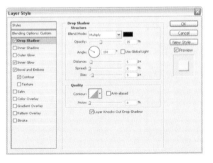

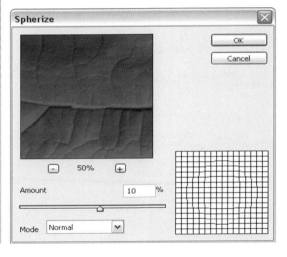

2 This is obviously a dried, fallen leaf but for this effect I wanted it to look bright and fresh. Although Photoshop has several commands available for changing one color into another, it can be useful to maintain more control. To manually change the color, start by creating a new layer above the image. Next, define a selection around the leaf, and, with the new layer active, fill the selection with a dark green color. Finally, set the blending mode of the layer to *Hard Light*. This color layer can be adjusted at any time as desired. When happy with the result, flatten the image.

4 Since water droplets behave like miniature lenses, they magnify and displace the subject seen through them. To simulate this effect, Ctrl (Cmd) + click the water layer to select the droplets. Then, with the main leaf layer active, apply the *Spherize* filter from the *Filter > **Distort*** menu. In the *Filter* dialog, set the Mode to *Normal* and use a low value for the *Amount*.

ICICLES

Icicles and freezing weather are synonymous with deep winter, and you can transform a normal scene into a magical winter wonderland by adding your own digital icicles. The method shown in this project is straightforward and uses only one of the built-in Photoshop filters. For added realism, and to show how the technique can be made more versatile, we will make use of different selections and vary the number of times the Photoshop filter is applied to each part of the image.

As with all the projects in this book, it helps to think about how the real-world object of the exercise is formed and how natural light affects its appearance. Icicles often form after freezing rain during the night, appearing new and sparkling with the rising of the sun.

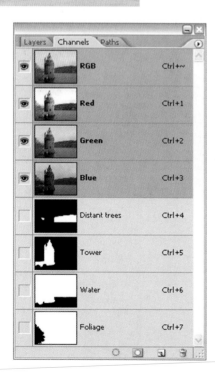

1 Start with an image depicting a winter scene, such as the lake view I've chosen for this project. Since the icicles need to be different sizes depending on where they are in the scene, start by making selections of the near, middle and far distant subject matter. Here I made selections of the foliage to the left, the tower, the water, and the distant trees, and saved these for later use.

2 We will use the *Stylize* > **Wind** filter to create our icicles using grayscale copies of the main image. Note that this filter acts on the lighter tones most and only applies the effect sideways. Let's start with the distant trees. Check the *Channels* palette to find the channel with the best contrast in the trees—in this case the red channel looks best. Click the red channel thumbnail and then press Ctrl (Cmd) + A followed by Ctrl (Cmd) + C to copy it to the clipboard. Now press Shift + Ctrl (Cmd) + N to make a new layer and press Ctrl (Cmd) + V to paste the grayscale image into the new layer. Now use *Levels* to increase the contrast of this layer.

3 Change the blending mode of the layer to *Hard Light*. Rotate the canvas using the *Image* > *Rotate Canvas* > **90° CW** command. Now apply the *Stylize* > **Wind** filter using the settings shown in the dialog. Since these trees are distant we can reduce the effect of the filter by immediately using the *Edit* > **Fade Wind** command (Shift + Ctrl (Cmd) + F). We can now use *Image* > *Rotate Canvas* > **90° CCW** to return the image to normal.

4 Now use the previously saved selection of the trees to add a layer mask. Use the *Select* > **Load Selection** command and choose the "Distant trees" channel from the drop-down list. Then use the *Layer* > *Layer Mask* > **Reveal Selection** command to add a layer mask based on the selection. Finally, restrict the icicle effect to the mid- to light tones by accessing the *Layer Style* dialog; double-click the layer thumbnail and slide the black triangle (Press the Alt (Opt) key to split the triangle as you drag it) under the *This Layer* scale to the left, removing the effect from the darker tones.

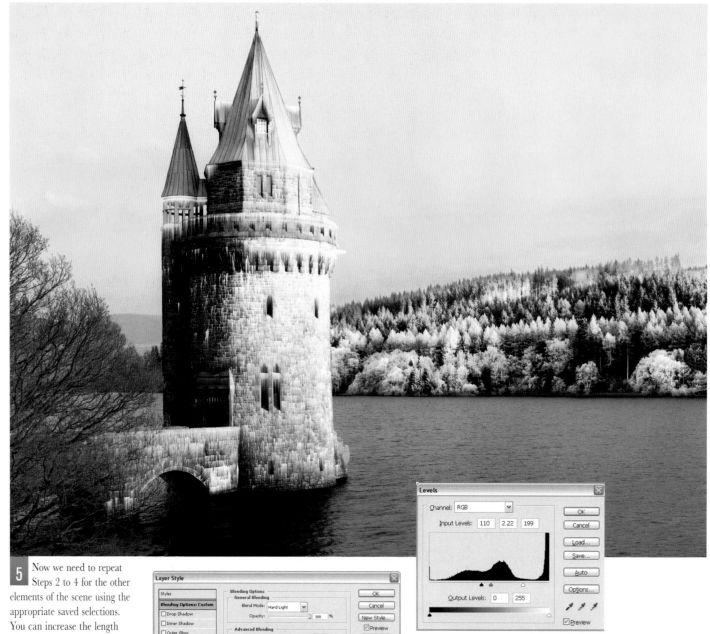

5 Now we need to repeat Steps 2 to 4 for the other elements of the scene using the appropriate saved selections. You can increase the length of the icicles by applying the *Wind* filter more than once. For the tower in this scene I applied the filter three times. Also, the layer options for this layer style will vary with each element, depending on the look you want. Once the layer mask has been added using the saved selection, you can modify it to control exactly where the icicles will be on the subject. For a building like this tower, reduce the effect from areas where icicles don't form—such as the sloping roof—by painting on the layer mask.

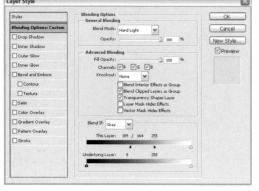

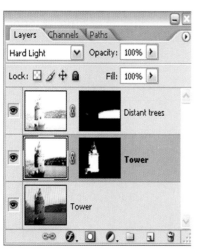

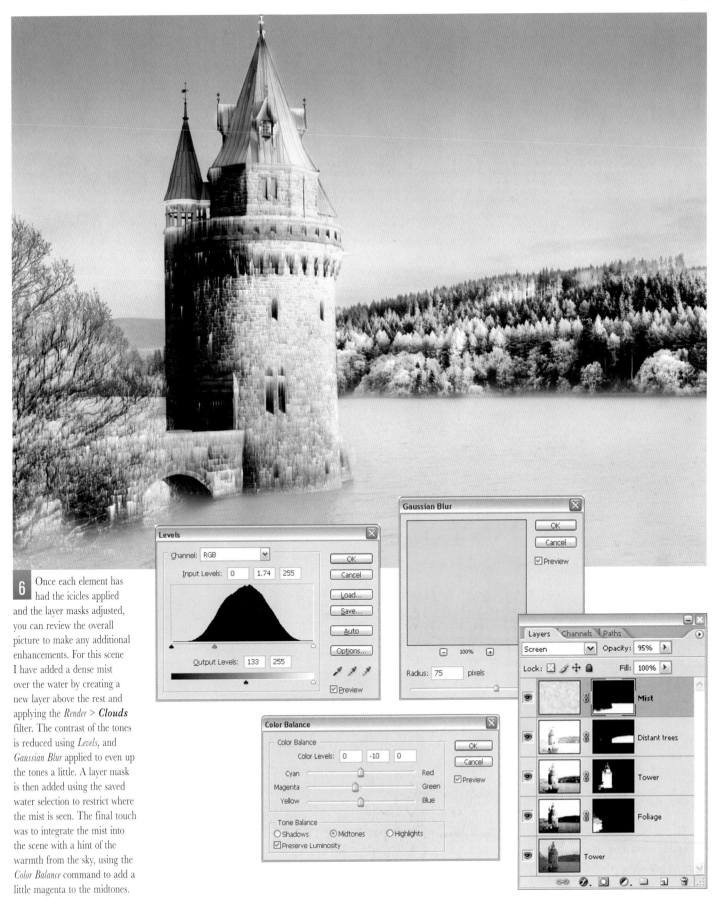

6 Once each element has had the icicles applied and the layer masks adjusted, you can review the overall picture to make any additional enhancements. For this scene I have added a dense mist over the water by creating a new layer above the rest and applying the *Render > Clouds* filter. The contrast of the tones is reduced using *Levels*, and *Gaussian Blur* applied to even up the tones a little. A layer mask is then added using the saved water selection to restrict where the mist is seen. The final touch was to integrate the mist into the scene with a hint of the warmth from the sky, using the *Color Balance* command to add a little magenta to the midtones.

CREATING SNOW

The appearance of winter snow is one of the most dramatic natural events, totally transforming the look and feel of the landscape. The most uninteresting scene can become a visual delight simply by adding a blanket of fresh white snow. However, in many countries snow is as rare as Halley's comet and so the opportunity to photograph snowy landscapes never arises.

This project comes to the rescue by demonstrating an easy method of creating realistic snow for any landscape picture. Using selections, adjustment layers, and a couple of standard Photoshop filters, it is relatively quick to execute depending on the complexity of the original image. For this example I have purposely chosen an image containing complex subject matter—the bushes and trees—to show just how effective the results can be.

1 Choose the image you wish to convert into a snowy landscape and make any basic corrections that may be required. For the starting image shown here I corrected the contrast and removed some unwanted flare from the back lighting.

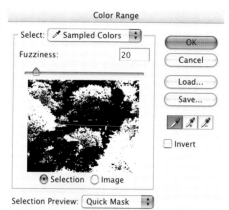

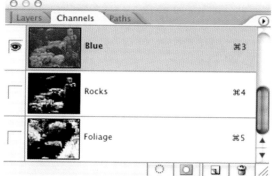

2 The initial step is to decide where you want the snow to be in the scene and then create selections of those areas for later use as masks. For this image I wanted to apply the snow to both the rocks and foliage and decided to make separate selections of each for greater control. Since the snow was to be applied mainly on the top and partly on the sides of the rocks, a very complex mask was needed. Instead of using the selection tools I used a quicker method. I copied the main image to a new layer, removed the color with the *Desaturate* command, and then used the *Levels* command to dramatically increase the contrast, removing all but the middle and light tones. Next, I cleaned up the mask using a black brush to remove any stray details. The result was finally copied and pasted into a new channel.

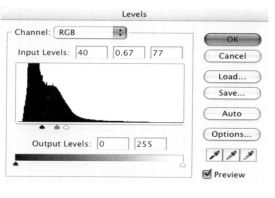

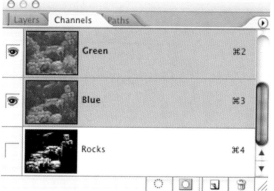

3 Since the foliage had good color and I wanted to include some of the shadow areas in the selection, I used the *Color Range* command. By sampling various colors from the foliage in the Color Range dialog it was easy to create a complex mask. I have shown the resulting selection here in *Quick Mask* mode so it is clear how complex the mask is. This selection was saved to a new channel and named "Foliage" using the *Select > Save Selection* command. If desired, fine-tune each of the individual masks in the *Channels* palette (this can be done later if required). The basic *Alpha* mask channels are shown in the screengrab.

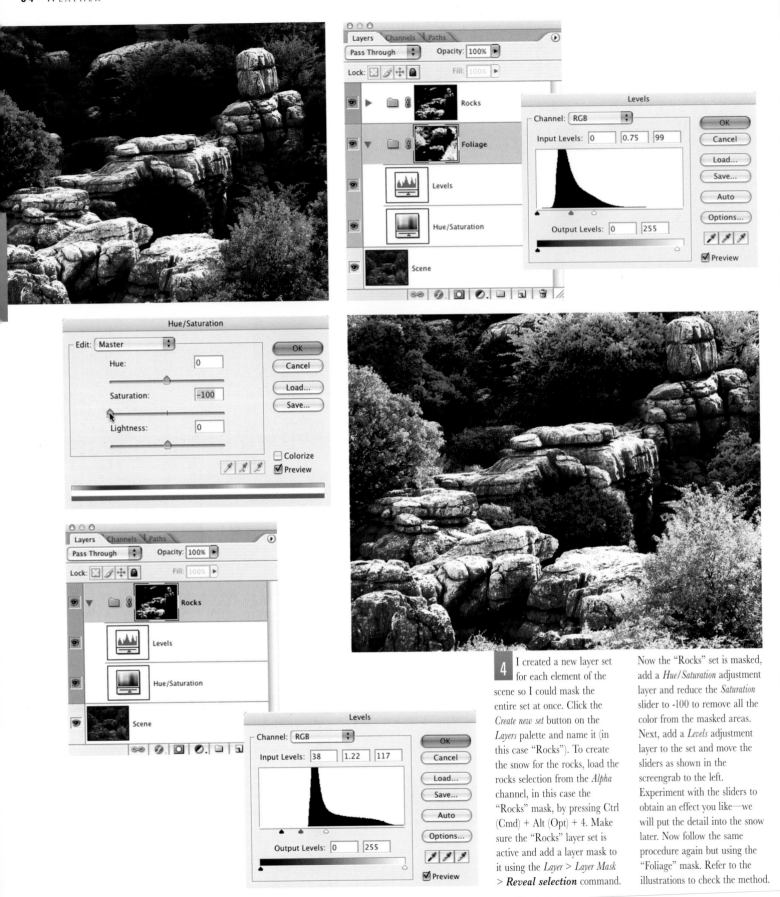

4 I created a new layer set for each element of the scene so I could mask the entire set at once. Click the *Create new set* button on the *Layers* palette and name it (in this case "Rocks"). To create the snow for the rocks, load the rocks selection from the *Alpha* channel, in this case the "Rocks" mask, by pressing Ctrl (Cmd) + Alt (Opt) + 4. Make sure the "Rocks" layer set is active and add a layer mask to it using the *Layer > Layer Mask > Reveal selection* command.

Now the "Rocks" set is masked, add a *Hue/Saturation* adjustment layer and reduce the *Saturation* slider to -100 to remove all the color from the masked areas. Next, add a *Levels* adjustment layer to the set and move the sliders as shown in the screengrab to the left. Experiment with the sliders to obtain an effect you like—we will put the detail into the snow later. Now follow the same procedure again but using the "Foliage" mask. Refer to the illustrations to check the method.

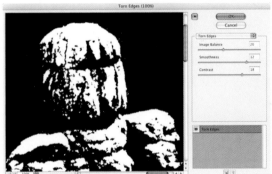

5 We now have our basic snow effect. To add some realism we need to roughen the edges of the snow and give it some texture. Make the "Rocks" layer set active and click on the layer mask. Now apply the *Sketch* > **Torn Edges** filter using settings similar to those shown here. This will roughen the edges of the snow. Now to add snow texture.

Load the "Rocks" mask by Cmd (Ctrl) + Clicking on the set layer mask and apply the *Sketch* > **Note Paper** filter. It is important to activate the "Rocks" selection so the texture is only applied to the snow. Experiment with the settings for both these filters to obtain the desired result. Now repeat this procedure for the "Foliage" layer set.

6 The final result has had minor adjustments made to the various set masks, and the *Opacity* settings of the *Hue/Saturation* layers were reduced to allow some of the original color to show through.

OVERCAST TO SUNSHINE

Ptotographs taken when the weather is overcast or the location is shady, such as in a dense wood, can suffer from low-contrast lighting which makes them appear dull and uninteresting. If your composition is captivating but the overall picture is let down by flat light, you can use Photoshop to simulate a more dynamic lighting mood. In this project, the image of the woodland scene shows the typical result of dull lighting. Although the composition is effective, the picture will be enlivened by using digital lighting techniques.

Save Selection

Destination

Document: Overcast to Sunshine

Channel: *New*

Name: Trees

OK

Cancel

Operation

● New Channel
○ Add to Channel
○ Subtract from Channel
○ Intersect with Channel

1 Start the project by making basic contrast corrections to the main image. We will be adjusting the tonal values of various elements in the image later, so don't overdo the basic correction.

2 For maximum flexibility it is a good idea to make selections of the important elements of the scene that we will be changing. Use the various selection tools to create individual selections of each element, and save each selection with a name using the *Select > Save Selection* command. Due to the similarity in tone and color of this scene's elements, I have used the *Quick Mask* mode to paint selections for each tree, the two foreground rocks, and the middle-distance rocks. The other areas can be selected by loading these saved selections in various combinations using the *Select > Load Selection* command.

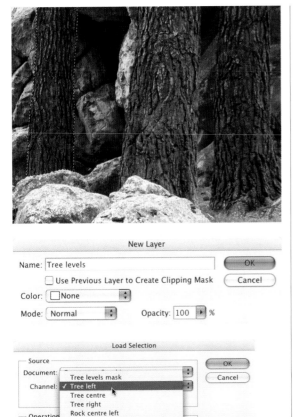

3 We will start by creating warm evening sunshine, entering the scene from the right and illuminating the trees. Add a new *Levels* adjustment layer above the main image and fill the attached layer mask with black. At this point do not adjust the *Levels* sliders, simply create the layer. Now load the selection for the first tree using the *Select* > **Load Selection** command.

4 Since we want to simulate side-lighting on the tree trunks, it is necessary to restrict the effect of the *Levels* adjustment using the layer mask and each separate tree selection. With the first tree selection active, click the *Levels* layer mask in the *Layers* palette. Use the *Gradient* tool to drag a white to transparent linear gradient horizontally from the right edge of the selected tree to half the width of the selection. Now double-click the *Levels* thumbnail and adjust the *Levels* sliders as desired. The right side of the selected tree will be affected by the levels changes simulating sunlight from the right.

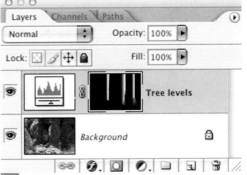

5 Repeat Step 4 for the other two trees by first loading each relevant selection and applying the gradient within the selection on the *Levels* layer mask. The lighting effect will be similar for each tree, but not exactly the same due to the tonal variations of the trees.

6 Load the selection of the middle-distance rocks and create a new *Levels* adjustment layer. This adjustment layer will be masked by the selection and so affect only the selected area. You can see the selected area in red in the screengrab.

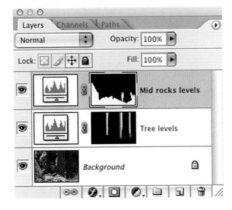

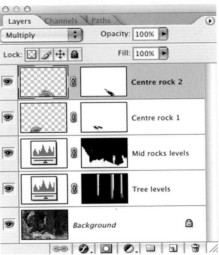

7 The two foreground rocks need a little more shadow to reinforce the impression of the lighting direction. Load the selection of one of the rocks and press Ctrl + J to create a new layer (A). Change the blending mode of the layer to *Multiply*—this darkens the rock (B). Now add a layer mask to the layer and paint onto the layer mask using a black brush, to lighten the right side of the rock (C). Repeat this procedure for the other central rock.

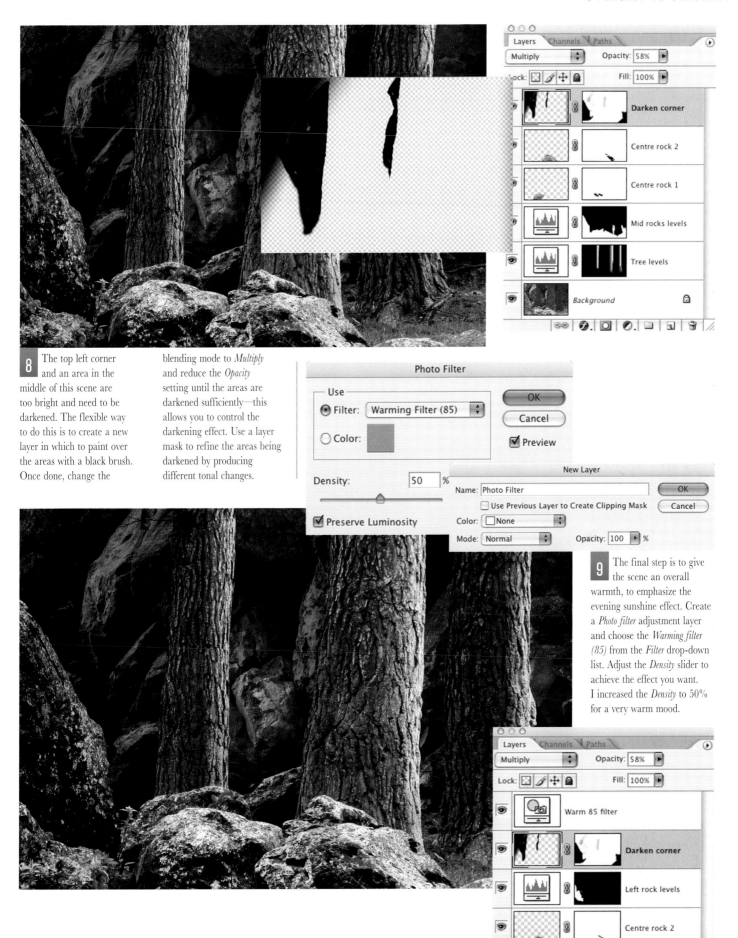

8 The top left corner and an area in the middle of this scene are too bright and need to be darkened. The flexible way to do this is to create a new layer in which to paint over the areas with a black brush. Once done, change the blending mode to *Multiply* and reduce the *Opacity* setting until the areas are darkened sufficiently—this allows you to control the darkening effect. Use a layer mask to refine the areas being darkened by producing different tonal changes.

9 The final step is to give the scene an overall warmth, to emphasize the evening sunshine effect. Create a *Photo filter* adjustment layer and choose the *Warming filter (85)* from the *Filter* drop-down list. Adjust the *Density* slider to achieve the effect you want. I increased the *Density* to 50% for a very warm mood.

CREATING RAINBOWS

Rainbows are almost impossible to anticipate when making landscape pictures, and even harder to capture successfully with a camera. Real rainbows are produced by the refraction of sunlight as it passes through small droplets of water in the atmosphere. This usually occurs when the sun dips below rain clouds just as light rain is falling. The stronger the sunlight, the more brilliant and saturated the rainbow. The effect is further enhanced by a backdrop of dark storm clouds.

Since real rainbows are so difficult to capture, it is much easier to produce them in the controlled, digital environment of Photoshop. The secret to producing convincing results is to ensure the image also contains the other natural elements, as described above, that are present when rainbows are seen in nature. The following project shows one way to achieve a natural rainbow image.

1 For best results start with an image that is lit by afternoon sunlight, as shown here. If the sky is clear, as is often the case on warm afternoons, it will be necessary to add a more moody, cloudy sky.

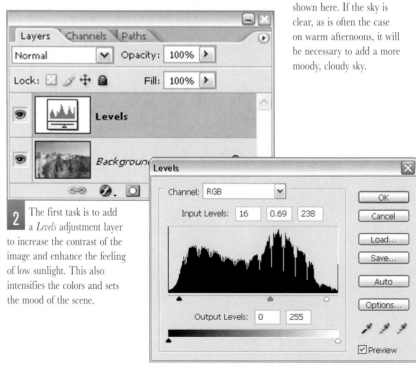

2 The first task is to add a *Levels* adjustment layer to increase the contrast of the image and enhance the feeling of low sunlight. This also intensifies the colors and sets the mood of the scene.

New Gradient…

Rename Gradient…
Delete Gradient

Text Only
✓ Small Thumbnail
Large Thumbnail
Small List
Large List

Preset Manager…

Reset Gradients…
Load Gradients…
Save Gradients…
Replace Gradients…

Color Harmonies 1
Color Harmonies 2
Metals
Noise Samples
Pastels
Simple
Special Effects
Spectrums

3 To add the storm clouds often seen as the backdrop to a rainbow, copy some rain clouds from another image to a new layer above the main scene. Use the *Edit > Transform > Scale* command to adjust the "Clouds" layer as needed. Next, select the skyline of the original scene and use it to add a layer mask to the clouds layer. If necessary, adjust the tonal values of the cloud layer using *Levels* to produce the desired mood.

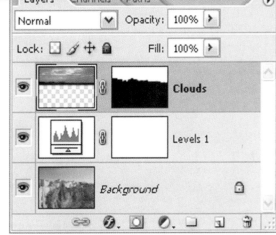

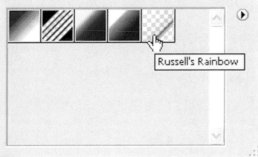

Russell's Rainbow

4 Before creating the rainbow we need to load a special gradient. Click on the *Gradient* tool and open the *Gradients* palette. Click the *Palette menu* button and choose *Special Effects* to load a new set of gradients. Select *Russell's Rainbow* from the available gradients. You could use this gradient as it is, but I felt there was too much blue and decided to edit the gradient for a more pleasing result.

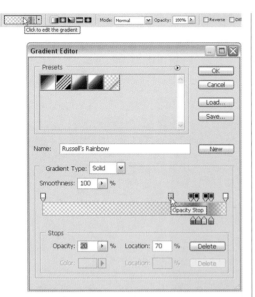

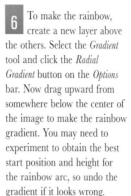

6 To make the rainbow, create a new layer above the others. Select the *Gradient* tool and click the *Radial Gradient* button on the *Options* bar. Now drag upward from somewhere below the center of the image to make the rainbow gradient. You may need to experiment to obtain the best start position and height for the rainbow arc, so undo the gradient if it looks wrong.

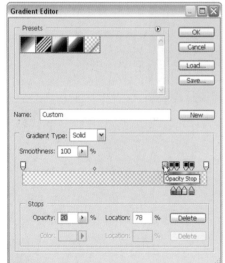

5 To edit the gradient, click on the gradient in the *Options* bar. This opens the *Gradient Editor* where you can make changes to an existing gradient or define a new one. To reduce the blue in the gradient simply change the position of the *Opacity* stop as shown in the screengrabs. Click *OK* when you're done.

7 When the rainbow looks good you can use the *Edit > Transform > Scale* command to adjust its size, and the *Move* tool to position it accurately. When resizing the rainbow, hold the Shift key down and drag a corner handle to maintain a true circular arc. To make the rainbow more realistic set the layer blending mode to *Screen* and reduce the *Opacity* as desired. After seeing the rainbow I decided it needed to be more of an arc, so I increased the canvas size and scaled the sky and rainbow to give a better composition.

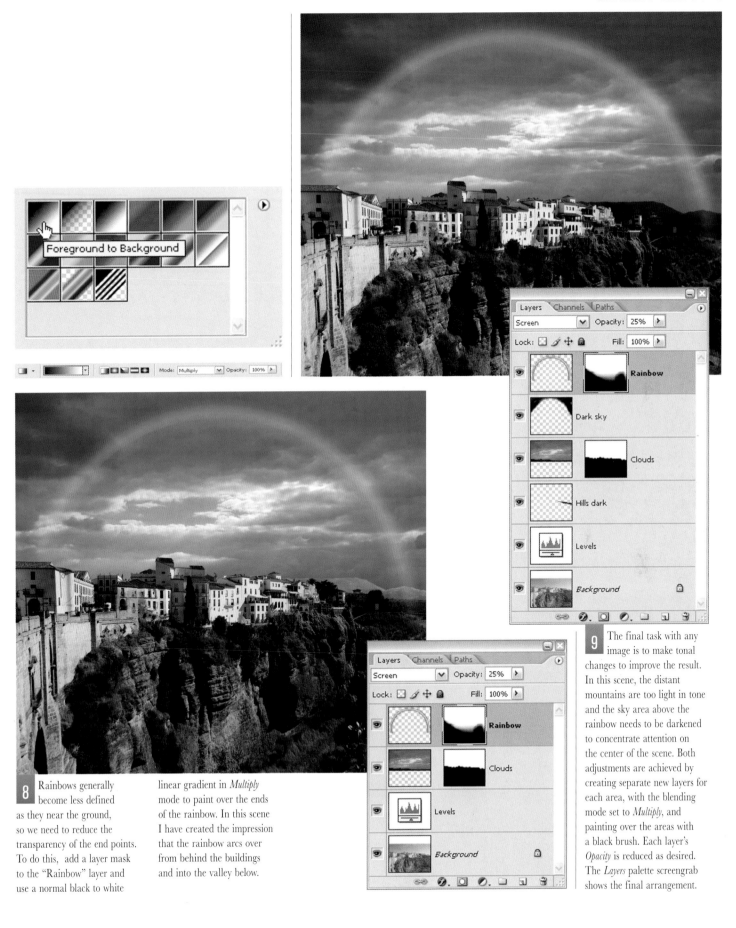

8 Rainbows generally become less defined as they near the ground, so we need to reduce the transparency of the end points. To do this, add a layer mask to the "Rainbow" layer and use a normal black to white linear gradient in *Multiply* mode to paint over the ends of the rainbow. In this scene I have created the impression that the rainbow arcs over from behind the buildings and into the valley below.

9 The final task with any image is to make tonal changes to improve the result. In this scene, the distant mountains are too light in tone and the sky area above the rainbow needs to be darkened to concentrate attention on the center of the scene. Both adjustments are achieved by creating separate new layers for each area, with the blending mode set to *Multiply*, and painting over the areas with a black brush. Each layer's *Opacity* is reduced as desired. The *Layers* palette screengrab shows the final arrangement.

WIND

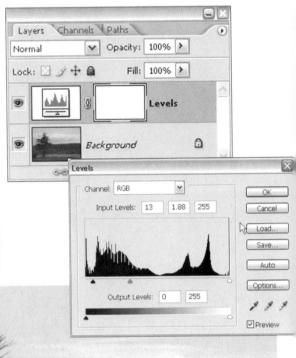

Wind has traditionally been the worst enemy of the landscape photographer when it comes to producing sharp images. However, the wind is one of nature's most potent forces, whether it is a light but persistent coastal breeze, or concentrated into a raging hurricane or twisting tornado. The more subtle and long-term effects of wind on the landscape can often be seen in the way trees and plants react to its presence. Trees in particular often show the effects of prolonged wind activity in the way they grow. The boughs will bend and curve as they grow to follow the wind's direction. Over time, the whole tree may be shaped into a permanent reminder of the potent effect of wind on our landscape. We can recreate this phenomenon with our own images of trees using Photoshop's specialized filters.

1 We start with a landscape where a tree is the primary subject, as shown here. The first step is to correct the contrast and color balance of the image using a Levels adjustment layer. Click the *Create new adjustment layer* button on the *Layers* palette. In the *Levels* dialog, correct overall contrast and tone using the *RGB* channel. To correct the heavy blue color cast and restore the foliage color, choose the Blue channel from the *Channels* drop-down list and adjust as necessary.

4 With the "Tree top" layer active, choose the *Filter > Distort > **Shear*** command. In the *Shear* dialog, click on the *Repeat Edge Pixels* option, then use your mouse to drag on the line to change its shape as shown. The preview area will show how the filter is affecting the tree. Click *OK* when ready.

2 The *Levels* changes we made have been applied to the entire image, but this has resulted in the sky becoming too light. To correct this, click on the *Levels* layer mask thumbnail and then use a soft black brush to paint over the sky area. Once you are happy with the changes, flatten the image.

5 Note how the tree is now misaligned. Use the *Move* tool to shift the "Tree top" image a little to the right.

3 Use the *Lasso* tool to make a rough, feathered selection around the branches. Set the *Feather* value in the *Lasso* options bar to 10 pixels. Include a generous amount of sky as this will be useful later. Press Ctrl (Cmd) + J to create a copy of the selection on a new layer above the original. Rename the layer "Tree top".

6 Duplicate the "Tree top" layer by dragging the layer thumbnail to the *Create a new layer* button on the *Layers* palette. Rename this copy layer "Tree top blur." Now apply the *Filter > Blur > **Motion Blur*** filter to create a small amount of side-to-side blur for the tree. Reduce the *Opacity* of the blur layer to 70% to combine it with the sharp layer underneath for a subtle wind effect. As a final touch, add a layer mask to the "Tree top blur" layer and use it to hide any unwanted blur on the background sky and trees.

MAKING A TORNADO

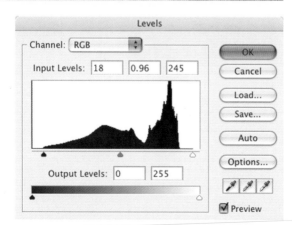

Tornadoes can be a devastating weather event, creating an awe-inspiring spectacle of destructive power. Capturing a tornado with a camera is both very difficult and very dangerous. Since it is very difficult to predict just when and where a tornado will occur, most photographers will never have the opportunity to produce a tornado picture.

It is useful to study pictures of real tornadoes to get an idea of how they look and the effect they have on their surroundings. Since tornadoes come in all sorts of shapes and sizes there is no one right way of depicting them. This makes it both easier and, at the same time, more difficult to simulate one since it largely depends on individual interpretation. This project will show you one way to produce a convincing simulation of a tornado and its destructive nature.

1 Tornadoes usually occur over relatively flat landscapes or open plains where there are few obstacles to prevent winds building to the high speeds associated with the phenomenon. We will start with just such an open scene. The first task is to correct tone and color using a *Levels* adjustment.

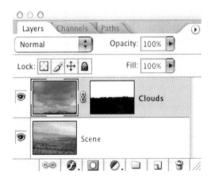

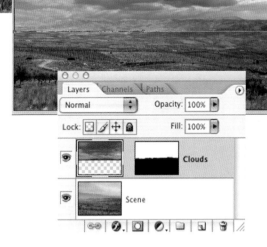

3 The "Clouds" layer needs to be scaled to fit the sky area—but before doing so make sure you unlink the layer mask from the "Clouds" layer. Click the *Chain* icon between the thumbnails of the "Clouds" layer in the *Layers* palette, or you will inadvertently scale the mask as well. Now use the *Transform > Scale* command from the *Edit* menu and drag the bottom handle upward until the clouds are correctly sized above the scene.

2 We need to change the sky in this scene, so copy a dramatic, low-altitude cloud formation from another image onto a new layer above the scene. Name the layer "Clouds." Make a feathered selection of the original sky with the *Magic Wand* tool and use it to add a layer mask to the "Clouds" layer. Now we can see the plains below the clouds.

4 Now to adjust the overall mood of the scene. The tones of the distant mountains need altering, so make a new blank layer above the scene layer and name it "Hill burn." Use the *Gradient* tool with a black to transparent linear gradient and drag down from just above the mountain tops to where the plain begins. Change the blending mode to *Multiply* and reduce the *Opacity* to 65%.

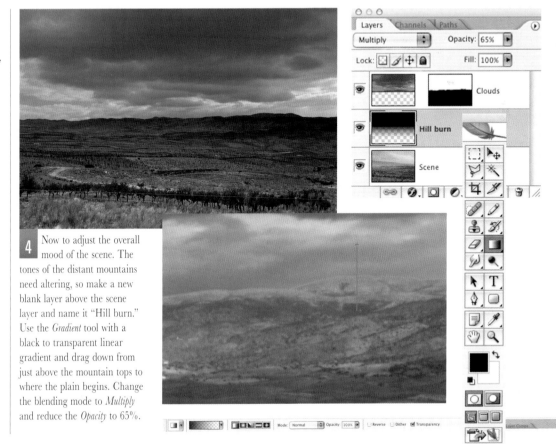

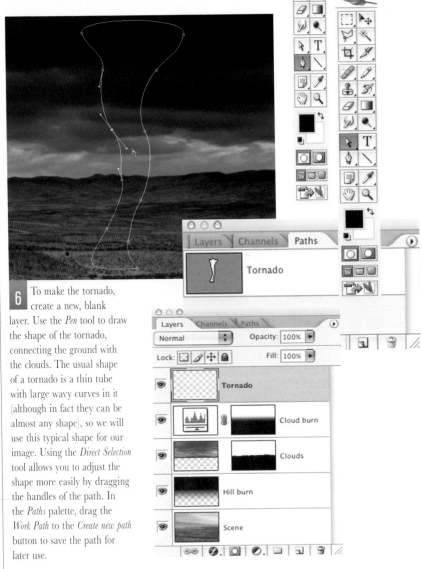

6 To make the tornado, create a new, blank layer. Use the *Pen* tool to draw the shape of the tornado, connecting the ground with the clouds. The usual shape of a tornado is a thin tube with large wavy curves in it (although in fact they can be almost any shape), so we will use this typical shape for our image. Using the *Direct Selection* tool allows you to adjust the shape more easily by dragging the handles of the path. In the *Paths* palette, drag the *Work Path* to the *Create new path* button to save the path for later use.

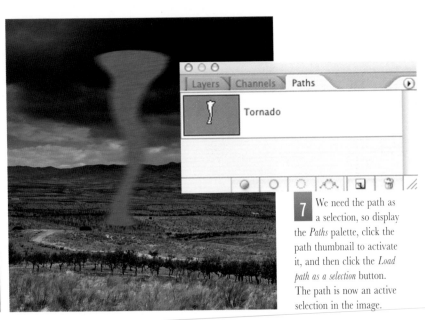

5 The clouds associated with tornadoes are usually huge and dark enough to block out the sun. To give our clouds the right mood, add a *Levels* adjustment layer above the "Clouds" layer and darken the clouds. Click on the layer mask thumbnail of the *Levels* layer and select the *Gradient* tool with a black to white linear gradient. Drag a gradient a short distance upward from just above the mountain tops to restrict the effect of the *Levels* adjustment solely to the clouds. The screengrab shows the mask in red. We have now set the right mood for the tornado.

7 We need the path as a selection, so display the *Paths* palette, click the path thumbnail to activate it, and then click the *Load path as a selection* button. The path is now an active selection in the image.

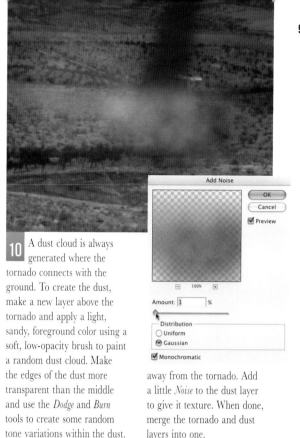

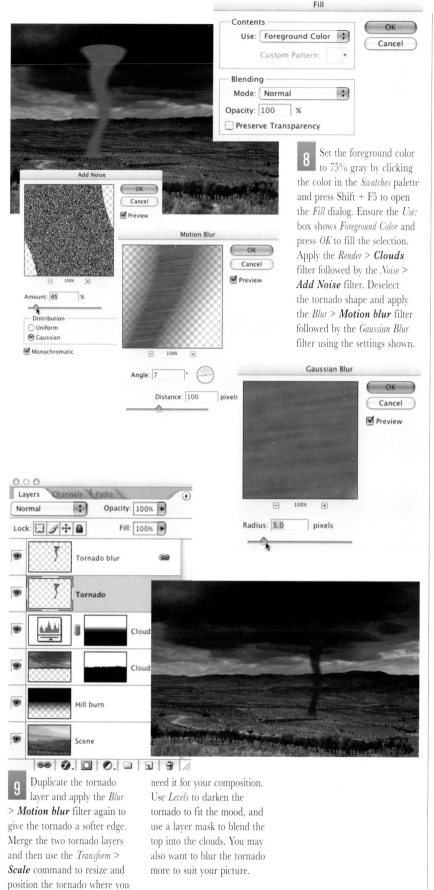

8 Set the foreground color to 75% gray by clicking the color in the *Swatches* palette and press Shift + F5 to open the *Fill* dialog. Ensure the *Use:* box shows *Foreground Color* and press *OK* to fill the selection. Apply the *Render > **Clouds*** filter followed by the *Noise > **Add Noise*** filter. Deselect the tornado shape and apply the *Blur > **Motion blur*** filter followed by the *Gaussian Blur* filter using the settings shown.

10 A dust cloud is always generated where the tornado connects with the ground. To create the dust, make a new layer above the tornado and apply a light, sandy, foreground color using a soft, low-opacity brush to paint a random dust cloud. Make the edges of the dust more transparent than the middle and use the *Dodge* and *Burn* tools to create some random tone variations within the dust. Secondly, paint a sandy-colored trail on the ground leading away from the tornado. Add a little *Noise* to the dust layer to give it texture. When done, merge the tornado and dust layers into one.

9 Duplicate the tornado layer and apply the *Blur > **Motion blur*** filter again to give the tornado a softer edge. Merge the two tornado layers and then use the *Transform > **Scale*** command to resize and position the tornado where you need it for your composition. Use *Levels* to darken the tornado to fit the mood, and use a layer mask to blend the top into the clouds. You may also want to blur the tornado more to suit your picture.

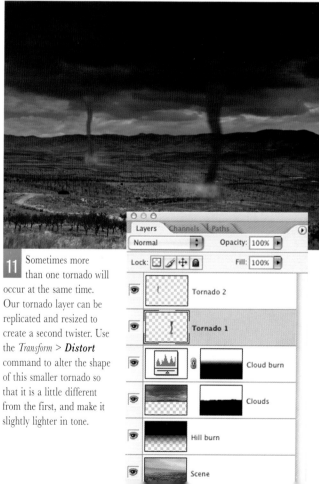

11 Sometimes more than one tornado will occur at the same time. Our tornado layer can be replicated and resized to create a second twister. Use the *Transform > **Distort*** command to alter the shape of this smaller tornado so that it is a little different from the first, and make it slightly lighter in tone.

DAY TO NIGHT

1 Since we are simulating a night scene lit by a full moon, objects in the final picture will need fairly strong, sharp shadows. To facilitate the desired result I have chosen a picture of a subject that is lit by strong directional sunlight to provide good shadows.

One of the most frustrating things about outdoor photography is finding yourself at a particular location at the wrong time of day for the result you desire. Once again digital manipulation comes to the rescue, perhaps allowing us to transform a daytime subject into the nighttime scene we originally had in mind. Before starting on this type of transformation it helps to understand the inherent visual qualities that characterize the type of scene we desire—whether it's a late afternoon, early evening, or moonlit night effect.

When deciding on a suitable subject to convert to a night scene, consider whether the shadows in the original scene will be sympathetic to the mood of the image you want to create. If they are, it will make the job far easier.

In this project we will change a normal daytime scene into a moonlit one and add other visual clues such as street lighting.

2 Since the original subject was photographed with significant convergence, the first step is to use the *Transform* > **Perspective** tool to reduce the distortion. It is also necessary to extend the foreground grass by increasing the canvas size a little and using the *Clone* tool to fill the new space with grass. This raises the horizon line, making a better composition. The picture is now ready to be converted into a night scene.

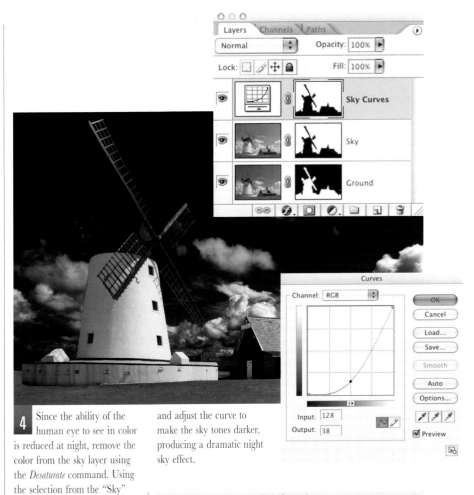

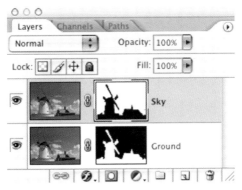

3 One way of working on a complex project is to make new layers of the main picture and use selections with layer masks to isolate the important parts of the image. Make the background layer into a normal layer by double-clicking on it, and name it. Now drag it to the *Create a new layer* button to make a copy, and rename this new layer. Next, to make the sky and buildings independent of each other, create a selection of the buildings and use it to add layer masks to each layer. Note in the *Layers* palette how the layer masks are opposites of each other—one for the sky and the other for the buildings. These are created from the same selection, which is inverted as needed.

4 Since the ability of the human eye to see in color is reduced at night, remove the color from the sky layer using the *Desaturate* command. Using the selection from the "Sky" layer mask (Ctrl [Cmd] + Click on the mask) to restrict the effect, add a *Curves* adjustment layer above the "Sky" layer and adjust the curve to make the sky tones darker, producing a dramatic night sky effect.

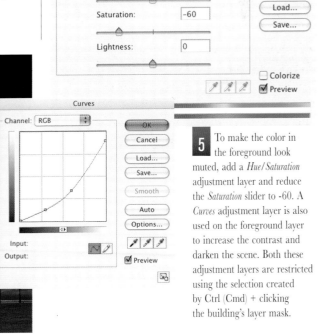

5 To make the color in the foreground look muted, add a *Hue/Saturation* adjustment layer and reduce the *Saturation* slider to -60. A *Curves* adjustment layer is also used on the foreground layer to increase the contrast and darken the scene. Both these adjustment layers are restricted using the selection created by Ctrl (Cmd) + clicking the building's layer mask.

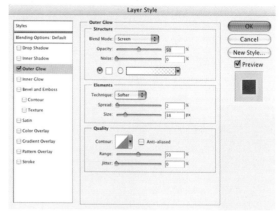

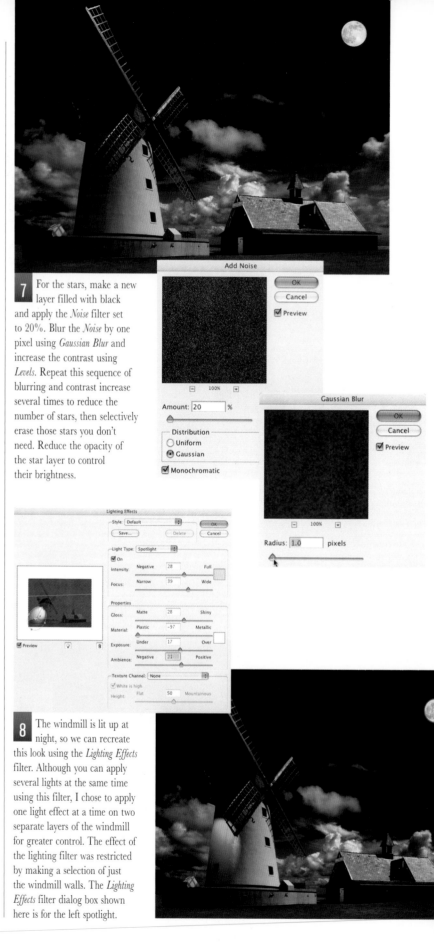

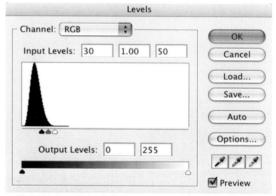

7 For the stars, make a new layer filled with black and apply the *Noise* filter set to 20%. Blur the *Noise* by one pixel using *Gaussian Blur* and increase the contrast using *Levels*. Repeat this sequence of blurring and contrast increase several times to reduce the number of stars, then selectively erase those stars you don't need. Reduce the opacity of the star layer to control their brightness.

6 Now we'll work on the sky. Place an image of the full moon on a new layer above the other layers and adjust the contrast to make it look bright. Create a glow around the moon to simulate the flare you perceive when looking at a full moon. Use the *Outer Glow* layer style for full control of the glow effect.

8 The windmill is lit up at night, so we can recreate this look using the *Lighting Effects* filter. Although you can apply several lights at the same time using this filter, I chose to apply one light effect at a time on two separate layers of the windmill for greater control. The effect of the lighting filter was restricted by making a selection of just the windmill walls. The *Lighting Effects* filter dialog box shown here is for the left spotlight.

10 To make the floodlighting more apparent we can add a cone of light for each light source. Create a new layer, then use the *Polygonal Lasso* tool to draw a cone shape emanating from the left floodlight.

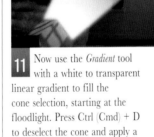

11 Now use the *Gradient* tool with a white to transparent linear gradient to fill the cone selection, starting at the floodlight. Press Ctrl (Cmd) + D to deselect the cone and apply a little *Gaussian Blur* to soften the edges of the beam. To merge the beam into the scene, change the layer blend mode to *Screen* and reduce the *Opacity* to 20%. Now repeat this process on new layers for the right floodlight and the street lamp on the right side.

9 Here we see the completed floodlighting on the windmill and simulated light from the street lamp at right. The street lamp light is created using feathered oval selections filled with a suitable color. Erase any unwanted color from the lamp light at the edges of the building.

12 As a final touch, apply a *Hue/Saturation* adjustment layer, with the *Colorize* option ticked, above the "Sky" layer to add a little silvery-blue color to the sky area. Use the sky selection to restrict the color. The screengrab of the layers palette shows the final order of the layers for this image.

CREATING A SUNSET

1 Although this scene has the necessary dramatic clouds and interesting light, the expected sunset colors simply did not materialize. It is necessary to add the final touch digitally.

Dramatic sunsets have to be one of the most beautiful natural sights people can witness, but for photographers, waiting for such an event to occur can be frustrating and disappointing. Traditionally, when the light isn't producing the desired result, various camera filters such as colored grads are utilized to add the required drama. Fortunately, using digital technology, almost any image can be transformed into a beautiful sunset by adjusting tonal values and adding warm sunset colors.

When creating a sunset, start with a scene that was photographed late in the afternoon, and preferably one that contains interesting clouds. Since dramatic sunsets largely depend on dramatic skies, this produces a better result. Also, the direction of the light should be similar to a natural sunset. Avoid scenes photographed in the middle of the day as the clouds will be lit from above, which is unnatural for a sunset.

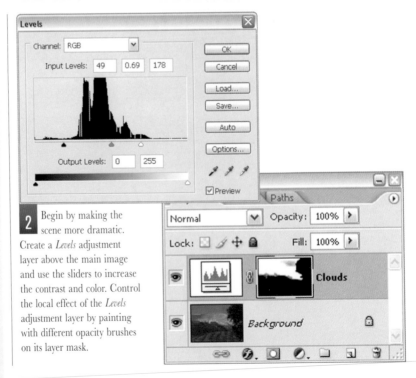

2 Begin by making the scene more dramatic. Create a *Levels* adjustment layer above the main image and use the sliders to increase the contrast and color. Control the local effect of the *Levels* adjustment layer by painting with different opacity brushes on its layer mask.

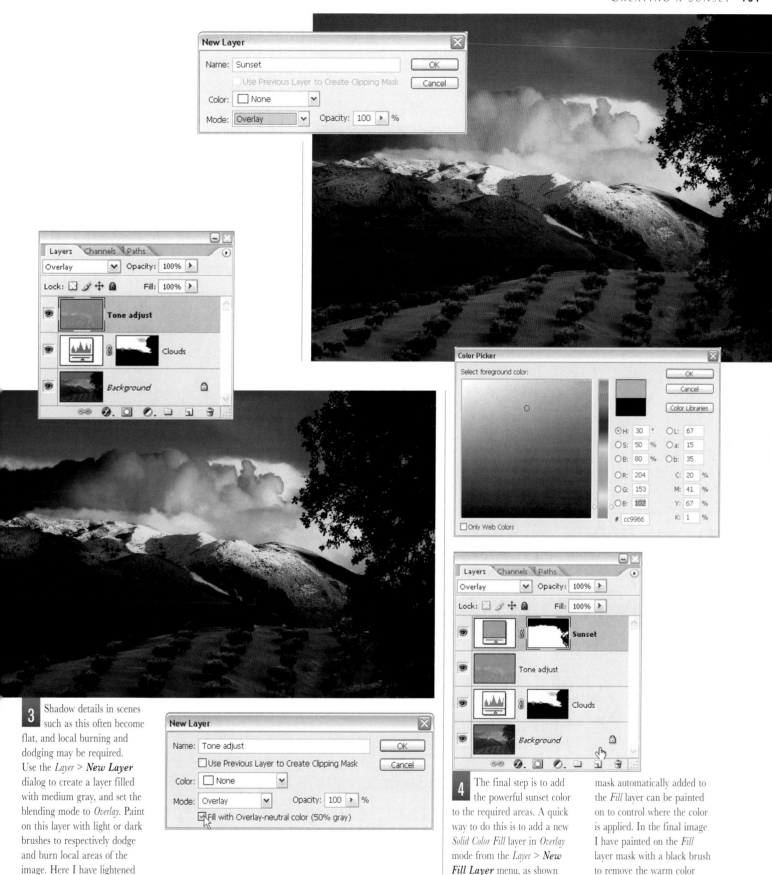

3 Shadow details in scenes such as this often become flat, and local burning and dodging may be required. Use the *Layer* > **New Layer** dialog to create a layer filled with medium gray, and set the blending mode to *Overlay*. Paint on this layer with light or dark brushes to respectively dodge and burn local areas of the image. Here I have lightened the tops of the rows of trees.

4 The final step is to add the powerful sunset color to the required areas. A quick way to do this is to add a new *Solid Color Fill* layer in *Overlay* mode from the *Layer* > **New Fill Layer** menu, as shown in the dialog boxes. The layer mask automatically added to the *Fill* layer can be painted on to control where the color is applied. In the final image I have painted on the *Fill* layer mask with a black brush to remove the warm color from the blue sky.

CREATING A MOONRISE

There are few sights more breathtaking than to see a large full moon rising above a mountain and glowing orange as it catches the last rays of the sun. This phenomenon, like so many other natural wonders, is easily missed: it only occurs in the winter months and lasts for just a few minutes. The presence of too much cloud, or the wrong choice of location, and the spectacle is lost from sight.

Since obtaining a good, high-quality photograph of a full moon is difficult, the answer is to create your own digital moon and add it to a suitable landscape picture. Follow the steps in this project and see how easy the process can be.

1 To make a digital moon, start by creating a new grayscale file of 6" x 6" (15 x 15cm) at 300 dpi. Since we need the moon to have a transparent background, make a new layer by clicking the *Create a new layer* button on the *Layers* palette.

New				
Name:	Moon			OK
Preset:	Custom			Cancel
Width:	6	inches		Save Preset...
Height:	6	inches		Delete Preset...
Resolution:	300	pixels/inch		
Color Mode:	Grayscale	8 bit		Image Size:
Background Contents:	White			3.09M
⌄ Advanced				

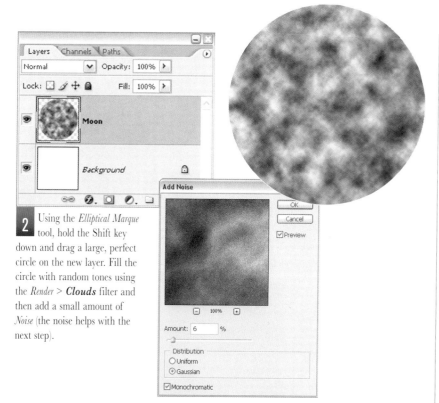

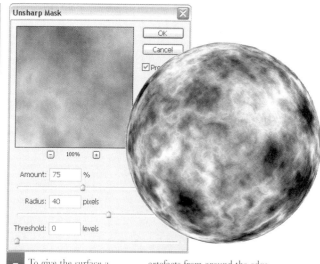

2 Using the *Elliptical Marquee* tool, hold the Shift key down and drag a large, perfect circle on the new layer. Fill the circle with random tones using the *Render > Clouds* filter and then add a small amount of *Noise* (the noise helps with the next step).

5 To give the surface a more gritty look, apply the *Unsharp Mask* filter twice using the settings shown. Finally, to remove some USM artefacts from around the edge, apply the *Distort > Spherize* filter one more time. The digital moon is now ready to add to a landscape image.

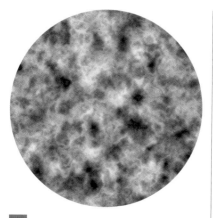

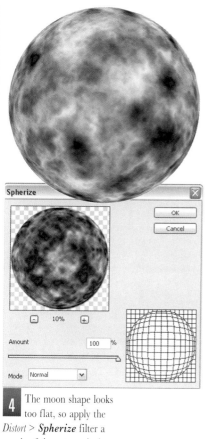

3 To create more detail for the moon surface apply the *Render > Difference Clouds* filter to the circle selection. The noise applied earlier helps the *Difference Clouds* filter to generate random lines and shapes to represent the craters and marks on the Moon's surface.

6 This late evening picture of a hillside village was taken just after sundown, exactly the time when a rising full moon catches the color of the sunset. The contrast and color balance of the image have been enhanced to create the right mood.

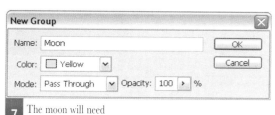

4 The moon shape looks too flat, so apply the *Distort > Spherize* filter a couple of times to make it appear rounded.

7 The moon will need several effects layers applied to it, so create a new Layer Set in the *Layers* palette and name it "Moon set."

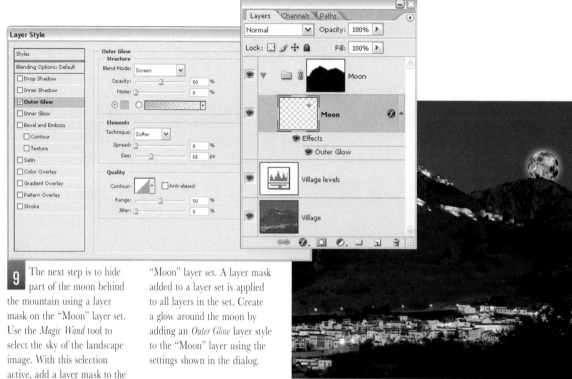

9 The next step is to hide part of the moon behind the mountain using a layer mask on the "Moon" layer set. Use the *Magic Wand* tool to select the sky of the landscape image. With this selection active, add a layer mask to the "Moon" layer set. A layer mask added to a layer set is applied to all layers in the set. Create a glow around the moon by adding an *Outer Glow* layer style to the "Moon" layer using the settings shown in the dialog.

8 With both the landscape and moon files open, drag the "Moon" layer from the *Layers* palette onto the landscape picture (hold the Shift key down as you drag, to center the moon on the new image). In the landscape's *Layers* palette, drag the new "Moon" layer into the Moon set. Now use the *Edit > Transform > Scale* command to make the Moon the desired size, and drag it into position.

10 We now have the moon masked, glowing and in position. Next we need to add some color and reduce the moon's contrast. First, Ctrl (Cmd) + Click the "Moon" layer to load it as a selection and then create a *Levels* adjustment layer above the "Moon" layer (the selection will create a layer mask). Reduce the contrast as shown in the dialog. Repeat the selection, this time creating a Solid Color Fill layer, and choose a warm color from the *Color Picker*.

11 Although the moon looks great, the composition needs something extra, so we'll add clouds from another image. Copy some interesting clouds to a new layer above the others. Use the *Hue/Saturation* command to make the color in the clouds more like a sundown effect.

12 Add a layer mask to the "Clouds" layer and paint with a black brush to hide everything but the clouds above the horizon line. Finally, to eliminate the excess sky tones, double-click the "Clouds" layer to open the *Layer Blend Options* dialog. In this dialog, remove the darker sky tones by adjusting the sliders on the *This Layer* scale.

CHANGING SUMMER TO FALL

The change of season from summer to fall is a wonderful time for photographers. The most dramatic indication of the onset of fall is that of leaves changing color on the trees. These changes can provide wonderful photographic opportunities— as long as you have access to the right scene.

Adobe Photoshop makes it easy to simulate this seasonal change for those not fortuntate enough to catch the fall colors in a natural setting. Photoshop has a useful command on the Image > Adjustments menu—the Replace Color command—that is just right for changing a specific color or a range of colors in an image. This project will demonstrate one method of changing the green leaves of summer into the mixed colors of a fall landscape.

1 Since fall is most often associated with the changing color of leaves on the trees, choose a summer image with plenty of trees.

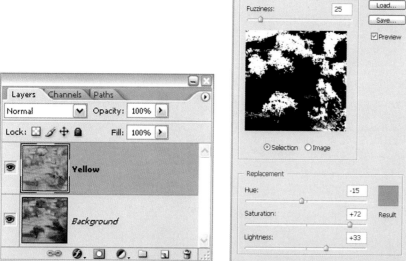

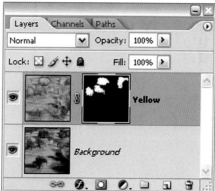

2 Copy the main image to a new layer and open the *Replace Color* dialog from the *Image > **Adjustments*** menu. Use the eyedroppers to select the colors in the image that are to be changed. In this example,

I have selected most of the foliage. Use the *Fuzziness* slider to control the spread. In the *Replacement* section, move the *Hue/Saturation* sliders to obtain a golden-yellow fall look, then click *OK*.

3 The *Replace Color* command selection has also included some other areas of the image in addition to the trees. These areas need to be hidden using a layer mask. We can mask out other trees at the same time, so we can apply a different color to them later.

4 To make the composition more interesting, and to simulate the way trees change color at different times, add a bright red color to some of the trees in the scene. To do this, simply repeat Step 2 using different values in the *Replace Color* command dialog.

5 Add a layer mask to the "Red" tree layer and hide those areas not required. The *Layers* screengrab shows the final arrangement. Change the blending mode of the "Red" layer to *Color* and the "Yellow" layer blending mode to *Screen* for more integration with the colors underneath. Adjust the *Opacity* of the layers as desired for a more subtle effect.

Photo Filter

Use

⊙ Filter: Warming Filter (85) ⌄

○ Color:

Density: 75 %

☑ Preserve Luminosity

OK

Cancel

☑ Preview

6 Finally, to give the image a feeling of warm light, add a *Photo Filter* adjustment layer above the original background image using the settings shown in the dialog screengrab.

DRAMATIC BEAMS OF LIGHT

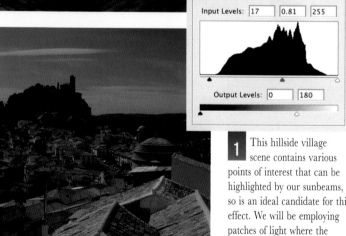

There is always something of a spiritual mood generated when the landscape is suddenly illuminated by strong beams of heavenly light radiating from a small break in an otherwise dark and brooding cloud formation. I always feel uplifted by such a sight and watch in awe as the light skims across the scene, highlighting different aspects of the land in its path.

The ability to simulate this effect in Photoshop is almost a "godsend" in itself. The technique is quite easy to do and its success or failure relies simply on the image you choose and how you compose the light rays to fit with the scene. In this project we exaggerate the gloom of a village scene rather more than might be found in reality.

1 This hillside village scene contains various points of interest that can be highlighted by our sunbeams, so is an ideal candidate for this effect. We will be employing patches of light where the beams will appear to strike the village, so start by using a *Levels* adjustment layer to reduce the contrast and darken the whole image.

Lighting Effects

Style: Default [▾]   OK
Save...   Delete   Cancel

Light Type: Spotlight [▾]
☑ On
Intensity: Negative 29 Full
Focus: Narrow 53 Wide

Properties
Gloss: Matte -41 Shiny
Material: Plastic 32 Metallic
Exposure: Under -15 Over
Ambience: Negative 25 Positive

Texture Channel: None [▾]
☑ White is high
Height: Flat 50 Mountainous

☑ Preview

3 Next, combine the effect of these two image layers by adding a layer mask to the "Lighting" layer. Paint on the layer mask with a soft black brush to hide all but those areas where the light beams will strike.

2 Now we want to give the impression of moody light from the left, so duplicate the original image to a new layer and apply the *Render > **Lighting Effects*** filter to produce a spotlight effect. Name this layer "Lighting."

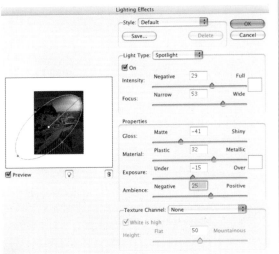

4 To introduce our dramatic sky, open a suitable image of clouds that are backlit by the sun and copy it to a new layer in the village scene. Then use the *Edit > Transform > **Distort*** command to introduce perspective and reshape the clouds to fit the scene. To integrate the clouds with the scene, make a selection of the original sky and use the *Layer > Layer Mask > **Reveal All*** command to add a masked layer mask to the "Clouds" layer.

5 To make a beam of light create a new blank layer and then use the *Polygonal Lasso* tool to draw the shape of your light beam, as shown here.

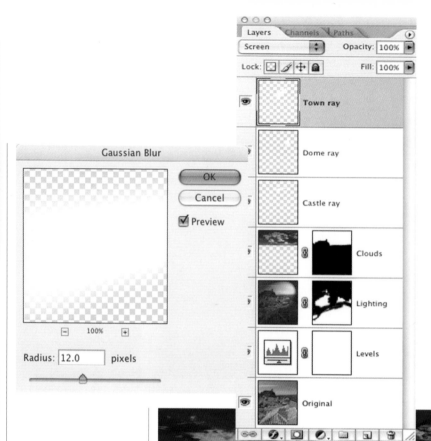

6 With this selection active, make the foreground color white (press X on your keyboard to switch colors), then, with the *Gradient* tool, drag a white to transparent linear gradient along the middle of the beam.

7 Create as many beams as you need, giving each its own layer to allow for individual adjustment. Select each "Beam" layer and soften its edges by applying *Gaussian Blur*. Finally, change the blending mode of each layer to *Screen* and reduce the *Opacity* setting as required. When you are happy with the beams, merge them into one layer.

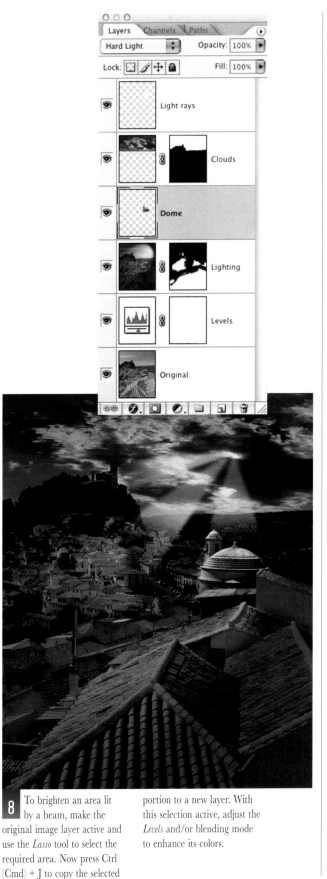

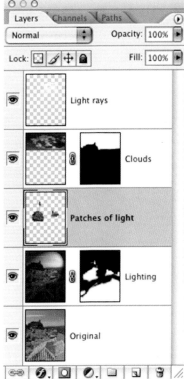

9 In this final version I have applied three beams of light, each striking a key feature of the village. This leads the eye from the foreground rooftops up to the castle on the hill, adding interest to the composition.

8 To brighten an area lit by a beam, make the original image layer active and use the *Lasso* tool to select the required area. Now press Ctrl (Cmd) + J to copy the selected portion to a new layer. With this selection active, adjust the *Levels* and/or blending mode to enhance its colors.

WATERFALLS

Waterfalls have always held a unique fascination for landscape photographers. The ever-changing shape and movement of the water, and the dramatic landscapes where waterfalls occur, combine to create intriguing visual imagery.

Photographing real waterfalls is often quite a challenge due to the difficulties of the location and the problems of water and equipment not mixing well. Fortunately, as this project will show, it is not too difficult to create a realistic and visually interesting image using the standard tools provided in Photoshop. By combining images of real elements and applying a little digital wizardry it is possible to create a "behind a waterfall" picture that in reality would be impossible for most people to achieve.

As with all the projects that attempt to recreate a natural phenomenon in this book, it is important to think carefully about the visual components that make up the effect in reality. When creating a digital waterfall consider how fast the water should move, how the natural light would affect the water, and whether the water is interacting with other objects in the scene. Observation of real waterfalls and incorporating little visual details will help add realism to an image.

1 Start with an image of a landscape where one might logically find waterfalls and caves. The rocky terrain in this picture is ideal since it has been formed by water erosion. Start by converting the background image into a normal layer by double-clicking it in the *Layers* palette. In the *New Layer* dialog, name the layer and press *Enter*. The first task is to use a *Levels* or *Curves* adjustment to define the contrast and color balance of the image. Here, I have accentuated the warm evening light and reduced the natural blue cast in the shadows.

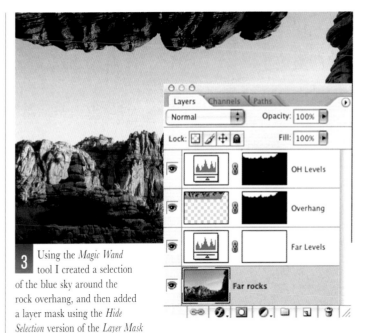

3 Using the *Magic Wand* tool I created a selection of the blue sky around the rock overhang, and then added a layer mask using the *Hide Selection* version of the *Layer Mask* command. Since the overhang was to represent the inside of a cave mouth it was necessary to darken both the color and tone of the rock using an adjustment layer. Before adding an adjustment layer, Ctrl (Cmd) + click on the "Overhang" layer mask to activate the mask as a selection. This selection will automatically add a layer mask to the adjustment layer so that it only applies to the overhanging rocks. The *Layers* palette screengrab shows the situation so far.

2 To create the view from within a cave opening, I copied a view of the rocks from another image and pasted it into a new layer. This image layer was then inverted and flipped using the *Edit > Transform* commands. The overhang image was flipped so that the direction of the light matched the background lighting. It is this attention to detail that makes for better images. Some perspective was applied to the rock overhang and it was then scaled until it looked natural.

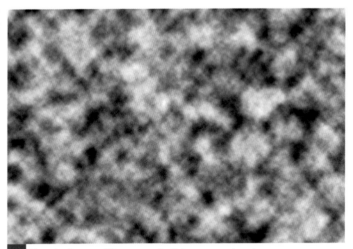

4 To make the waterfall, create a new layer and position it between the "Far rocks" and the "Overhang" layers so that the water will appear to come from above the rock overhang. Press the D key to reset the colors to black and white and use the *Filter > Render > **Clouds*** filter to generate a random pattern of tones. This will add tonal variation to the waterfall.

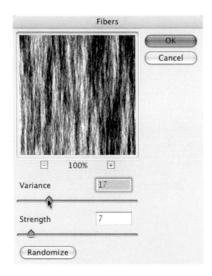

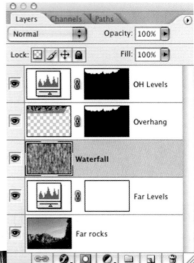

Feather Selection

Feather Radius: 50 pixels

OK

Cancel

6 To make the waterfall more interesting, add a layer mask to the "Water" layer and use the painting tools to produce a density mask. Think about how the water would naturally fall over the overhang, and vary the density of the water around the edges by painting on the mask layer with a large, soft brush. Vary the *Opacity* of the brush to achieve random water density. Creating various rectangular feathered selections and filling them using the *Gradient* tool can be useful.

5 Next, use the *Filter > Render > **Fibers*** filter to create the vertical flow of water. Changing the settings will produce different types of water effect, so select the settings according to the look you want. The settings I used are shown in the dialog box. To make the water interact with the main image, change the blending mode to *Screen*.

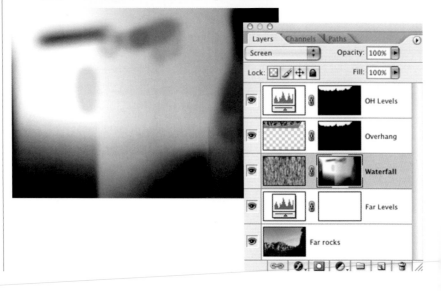

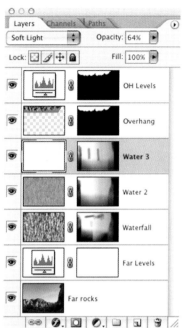

8 To add a touch of realism, I decided to create a light, misty effect just below the rock overhang to represent the spray as the water falls into space. On a new layer above the others, paint a random area around the edge of the overhang using a large soft brush and white and light-gray colors. The gray will add tonal variation when some *Gaussian Blur* is applied. Next, use the *Gaussian Blur* filter to soften the mist and reduce the *Opacity* of the layer until the effect looks right. If necessary, use a large eraser to modify the result.

7 To add more depth and variation to the waterfall I repeated the water creation process twice more on new layers, using different settings for the *Fibers* filter and different layer masks for each layer. I also used different blending modes—*Soft Light* and *Hard Light*—and individual *Opacity* settings to vary the way the layers interacted. This has given the waterfall more volume and a luminous appearance. The *Layers* palette screengrab above shows the new layers.

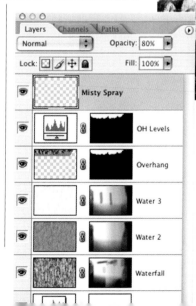

9 The final touch was to add a warm orange color using a large, soft brush at 50% opacity in *Overlay* mode to randomly paint on the main "Waterfall" layer. This added a subtle effect of evening light illuminating the waterfall.

LAKES AND RIPPLES

1 Sunset pictures are an ideal starting point for creating a digital lake; they contain a good variety of color and tone which will produce interesting reflections in the water. Start by double-clicking the "Sky" background layer to convert it to a normal layer, and name it "Sky." Drag the layer to the *Create a new layer* button on the *Layers* palette to create a duplicate, and rename it "Lake." Now invert this image layer with the *Edit > Transform > **Flip Vertical*** command.

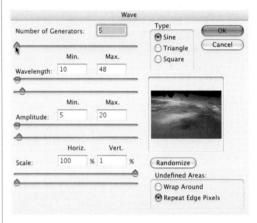

In landscape photographs, smooth lake surfaces represent tranquillity and the gentler side of nature. This atmosphere is often most effectively represented in the early evening when the wind drops and the scene undergoes the transition from day to night. You can set a slightly different tone with careful manipulation of reflections on the surface of a lake—an interestingly disturbed surface can hint at an eerie, mysterious mood.

In this project we will create a digital lake that is relatively still, with reflections on its surface. We will then add circular ripples similar to those that occur when a stone is thrown into the water, or a fish breaks the surface.

2 The surface of a real lake is never perfectly smooth, so it is necessary to introduce some distortion to our digital equivalent. Apply the *Distort > **Wave*** filter to the "Lake" layer using settings similar to those shown in the dialog. This will produce a gentle wave effect on the reflection of the sky.

3 To increase the realism of the lake surface, apply the *Distort* > **Ocean Ripple** filter to the "Lake" layer. Use low values in the *Filter* dialog so that the effect is subtle.

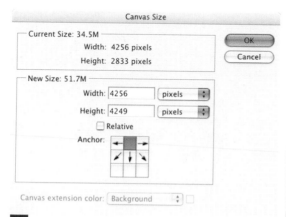

5 Now to position and reshape the "Lake" layer. Use the *Edit* > *Transform* > **Distort** command and drag the top center handle of the "Lake" layer down until the it meets the bottom edge of the "Sky" layer. Increase the width of the front edge too, to introduce realistic perspective into the lake's surface. When ready, hit the *Enter* key to activate the change.

4 Now we need to make room for our new lake by increasing the size of the canvas. Since the lake will be smaller than the sky (it's also good composition to have the horizon two-thirds of the way up the picture), make the height of the canvas 50% bigger, as shown in this *Canvas Size* dialog. Be sure to set the *Anchor* point as shown so the additional space goes at the bottom of the picture.

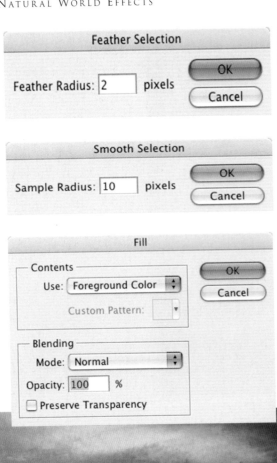

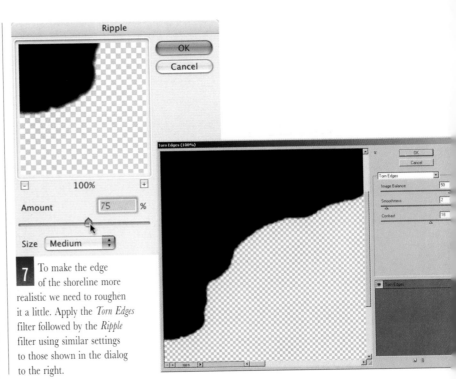

7 To make the edge of the shoreline more realistic we need to roughen it a little. Apply the *Torn Edges* filter followed by the *Ripple* filter using similar settings to those shown in the dialog to the right.

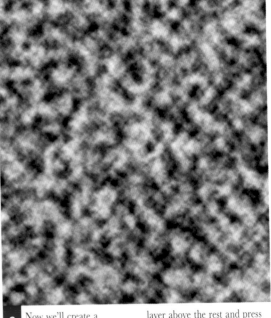

8 Now we'll create a radiating ripple effect on the lake surface to simulate the effect of a small stone tossed into the water. Create a new layer above the rest and press the D key to set the default colors. Apply the *Render > Clouds* filter to generate some random tones.

6 We need to give our lake a random shoreline rather than the straight line it has now. Use the *Lasso* tool to draw a random selection. If the line is too jagged, use the *Select > Modify > Smooth* command with a small sample radius of about 10 pixels. Once the selection is defined, press Ctrl (Cmd) + Alt (Opt) + D to open the *Feather Selection* dialog and apply a 2-pixel feather. With black as the foreground color, press Shift + F5 to open the *Fill* dialog and fill the selection. We now have our basic shoreline.

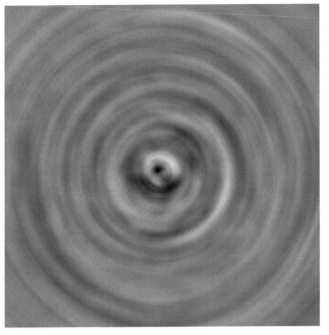

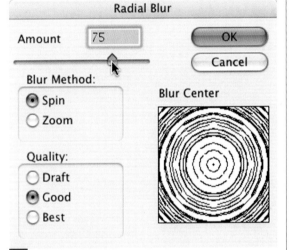

9 Next, apply the *Blur > **Radial Blur*** filter with the settings shown in the *Radial Blur* dialog. The result is an effective pond ripple appearance. Name this layer "Ripples."

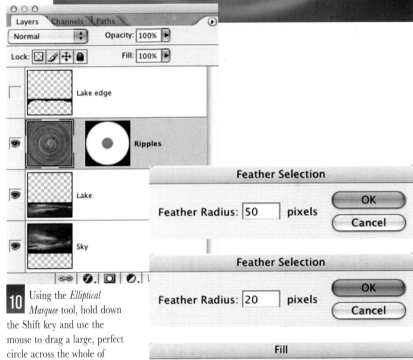

10 Using the *Elliptical Marquee* tool, hold down the Shift key and use the mouse to drag a large, perfect circle across the whole of the "Ripples" layer. Feather this circle selection using a large radius and then apply the Layer > **Layer Mask** command to the "Ripples" layer. With the layer mask active, make a smaller circle selection in the center of the ripples and fill it with 50% black to make the center semi-transparent.

Tip
The wind causes the surface of water in lakes to become turbulent—this can be simulated digitally by distorting any reflections on the water. When there is little turbulence, reflections from the scene on the water will be more accurate and detailed. As turbulence increases the reflections become less distinct, indicating the presence of wind in the scene.

11 The next task is to change the ripples so that they appear to be lying on the surface of the water. To obtain the correct perspective it is necessary for the ripples to have the same vanishing point as the lake's surface, so we need to create some guidelines to help produce an accurate result. Press Ctrl (Cmd) + R to make the rulers visible and drag a vertical guideline from the left ruler. Stop this guide where you want the center of the ripples to be placed. In this case it is positioned in the center of the image. Next, drag a horizontal guide from the top ruler and position it where the sky and lake join; this is our horizon line. Finally, create a new layer and use the *Line* tool to create two red diagonal guides from the bottom corners of the image to where the other two guides intersect.

12 With the "Ripple" layer active, initiate the *Edit > Transform > **Distort*** command and drag the corner handles onto the diagonal guidelines. This will create the correct perspective for the ripples. Reducing the height of the ripples determines their angle in relation to the scene, so ensure this fits with the surface of the lake.

13 To make our ripples a little more three dimensional, apply the *Sketch > **Bas Relief*** filter to the "Ripples" layer. Change the blending mode of the layer to *Soft Light* and reduce the *Opacity* as desired so the ripples merge with the water's surface. The final step is to darken the lake a little with a *Levels* adjustment layer, since a reflected image is never as bright as the original.

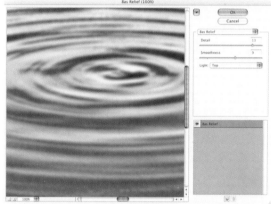

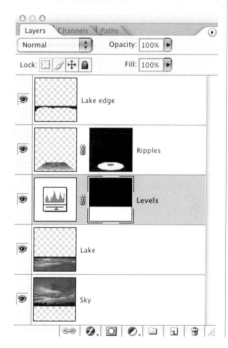

14 You can duplicate the "Ripple" layer several times and use the *Transform > **Scale*** command on each copy to create multiple ripples of varying size for your lake.

Two variations are shown here, one simulating a stone being skimmed across the lake, and the other simulating a group of overlapping ripples.

CREATING LIGHTNING

1 If you don't have a suitable or interesting composition of stormy clouds and landscape, simply combine two separate images. To the left and below we see the two images I have used to form the composite image for this project.

Savage storms that produce eye-scorching lightning bolts have a significant role in myth and folklore. People are fascinated by the spectacle of nature at its wildest, and there can be few things so exhilarating as forked lightning rending the sky from beneath dark, brooding clouds. Of course, capturing such a display with a camera is tricky, even for professional storm chasers, but with Photoshop at our command, producing such effects is within everyone's grasp.

In this project we will create some dramatic lightning, lending an ordinary landscape scene the excitement of nature in its rawest form.

2 With both image files open, double-click the landscape layer and name it "Land." Now copy the clouds image to a new layer in the landscape image and name it "Clouds." Make sure the lighting direction for both images is similar—if not, flip the "Clouds" layer horizontally.

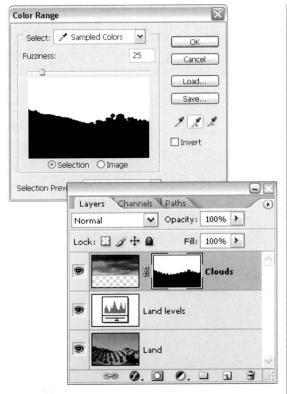

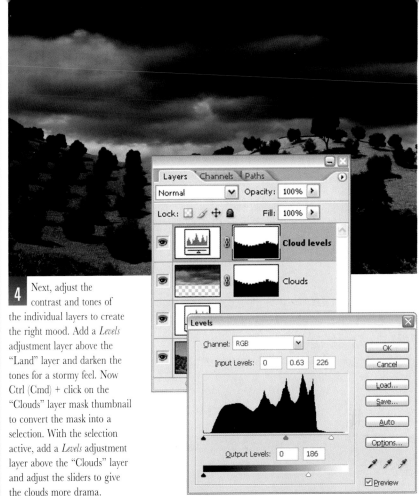

3 Create a selection of the blue sky using the *Color Range* command from the *Select* menu, and use it to add a layer mask to the "Clouds" layer. Adjust the mask as necessary. Here I have painted on the mask to hide some of the middle-distance hills in the landscape.

4 Next, adjust the contrast and tones of the individual layers to create the right mood. Add a *Levels* adjustment layer above the "Land" layer and darken the tones for a stormy feel. Now Ctrl (Cmd) + click on the "Clouds" layer mask thumbnail to convert the mask into a selection. With the selection active, add a *Levels* adjustment layer above the "Clouds" layer and adjust the sliders to give the clouds more drama.

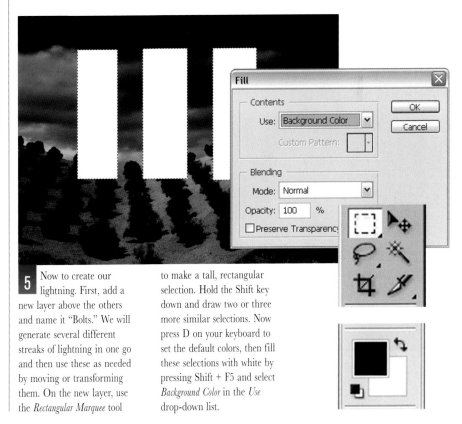

5 Now to create our lightning. First, add a new layer above the others and name it "Bolts." We will generate several different streaks of lightning in one go and then use these as needed by moving or transforming them. On the new layer, use the *Rectangular Marquee* tool to make a tall, rectangular selection. Hold the Shift key down and draw two or three more similar selections. Now press D on your keyboard to set the default colors, then fill these selections with white by pressing Shift + F5 and select *Background Color* in the *Use* drop-down list.

6 With the selections still active, choose a large, soft brush and paint half of each white box with black. Allow the lines to slope and bend in different ways for each box.

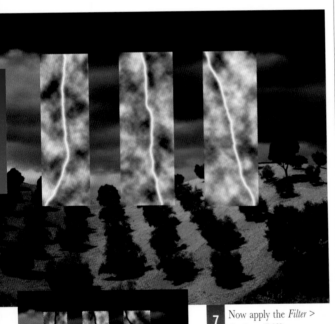

7 Now apply the *Filter > Render > Difference Clouds* filter to the boxes. This creates black lines which need to be white, so press Ctrl (Cmd) + I to invert the tones. You can now deselect the boxes by pressing Ctrl (Cmd) + D.

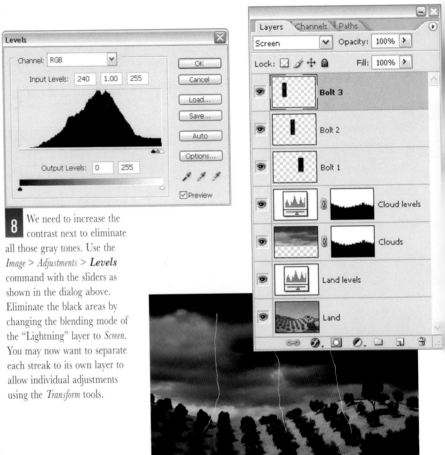

8 We need to increase the contrast next to eliminate all those gray tones. Use the *Image > Adjustments > Levels* command with the sliders as shown in the dialog above. Eliminate the black areas by changing the blending mode of the "Lightning" layer to *Screen*. You may now want to separate each streak to its own layer to allow individual adjustments using the *Transform* tools.

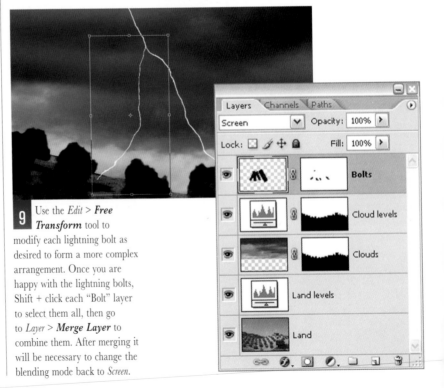

9 Use the *Edit > Free Transform* tool to modify each lightning bolt as desired to form a more complex arrangement. Once you are happy with the lightning bolts, Shift + click each "Bolt" layer to select them all, then go to *Layer > Merge Layer* to combine them. After merging it will be necessary to change the blending mode back to *Screen*.

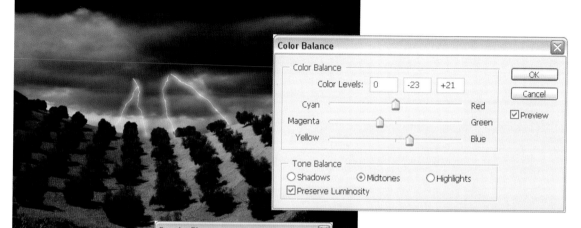

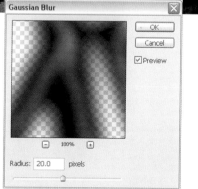

10 To make the lightning glow, duplicate the "Lightning" layer and apply some *Gaussian Blur*. I used an *Amount* value of 20, but this depends on your own image—just make it quite soft. Add a little color to the *Glow* by pressing Ctrl (Cmd) + B to open the *Color Balance* dialog, and move the sliders as shown on the right.

12 Finally, if desired, you can give the distant low cloud some light rain on a new layer in *Overlay* mode. Make a rectangular selection at the bottom of the clouds and fill it with a rain effect (the "Rain" project on page 72 shows you how to do this). Then use a layer mask to control the shape of the rain and the *Opacity* to control the density.

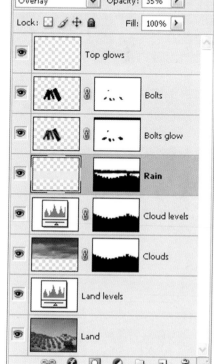

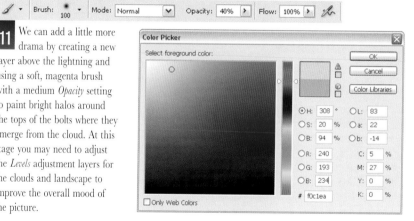

11 We can add a little more drama by creating a new layer above the lightning and using a soft, magenta brush with a medium *Opacity* setting to paint bright halos around the tops of the bolts where they emerge from the cloud. At this stage you may need to adjust the *Levels* adjustment layers for the clouds and landscape to improve the overall mood of the picture.

LUNAR LANDSCAPE

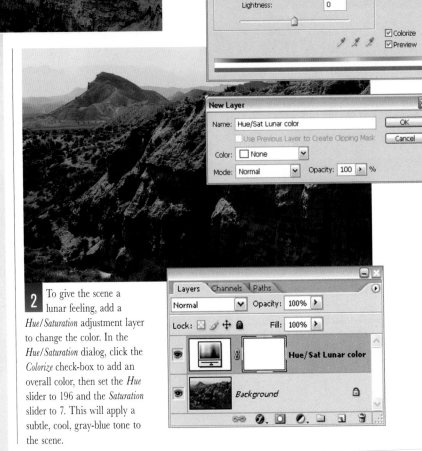

1 Start with a clean image and remove any unwanted detail with the *Clone Stamp* tool. Correct the contrast using a *Levels* adjustment.

Hue/Saturation

Edit: Master

Hue: 196

Saturation: 7

Lightness: 0

☑ Colorize
☑ Preview

OK
Cancel
Load...
Save...

New Layer

Name: Hue/Sat Lunar color

☐ Use Previous Layer to Create Clipping Mask

Color: ☐ None

Mode: Normal   Opacity: 100 ▶ %

OK
Cancel

Photographing a real lunar landscape can only be a dream for most of us, so the only way to reproduce one is to simulate the effect in Photoshop. Obviously, any landscape photograph taken on Earth will have qualities totally different to those of a lunar landscape. The most noticeable difference is the presence of atmospheric haze, which is evident in all normal landscapes to varying degrees. Real lunar landscapes have no atmosphere, so they appear very crisp and sharp all the way to the horizon. It is virtually impossible to simulate this effect precisely.

However, in this project we will see how to convert an arid, desert picture into something approaching the mood and feel of a lunar landscape.

Layers Channels Paths

Normal   Opacity: 100% ▶

Lock: ☐ ✎ ✛ ⬛   Fill: 100% ▶

👁 Hue/Sat Lunar color

👁 Background

2 To give the scene a lunar feeling, add a *Hue/Saturation* adjustment layer to change the color. In the *Hue/Saturation* dialog, click the *Colorize* check-box to add an overall color, then set the *Hue* slider to 196 and the *Saturation* slider to 7. This will apply a subtle, cool, gray-blue tone to the scene.

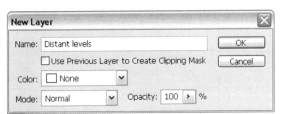

3 Now we need to reduce the distant haze in order to give the background more contrast, making it more prominent in the scene. The faint hills from the left at the horizon are detracting from the shape of the central mountain, so they will be removed. Add a *Levels* adjustment layer above the background image layer, and in the dialog move the tone sliders as shown to the right. Note that the white slider has been moved well into the graph to eliminate the clouds and the far distant hills. We will be adding a different sky effect later.

4 The *Levels* adjustment in Step 3 is currently affecting the whole image, so we need to paint on the attached layer mask to hide those areas of the scene we do not want the adjustment to affect. Use a black brush with different *Opacity* settings to control how the *Levels* affect different parts of the image. Painting with full black on the layer mask, as shown to the right, prevents any adjustment taking place in that area.

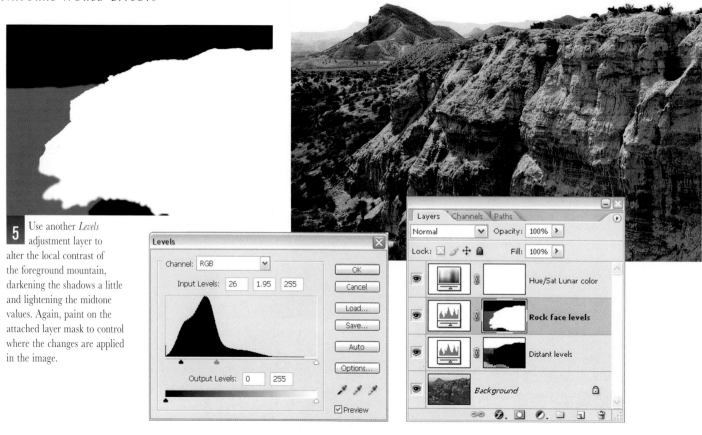

5 Use another *Levels* adjustment layer to alter the local contrast of the foreground mountain, darkening the shadows a little and lightening the midtone values. Again, paint on the attached layer mask to control where the changes are applied in the image.

6 Now to create a new sky. Make sure the default colors of black and white are set by pressing D on your keyboard. Next, add a new blank layer above the others named "Sky burn" and select the *Gradient* tool. In the *Options* bar, click on the small arrow next to the gradient and choose the *Foreground to Transparent* linear gradient. Start the gradient about one third of the way into the sky above the horizon and drag downward to just below the lowest point on the horizon.

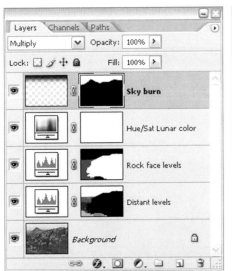

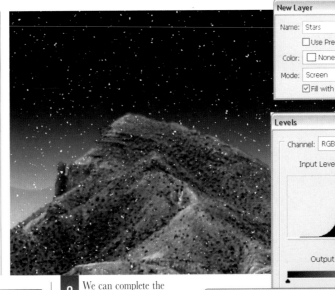

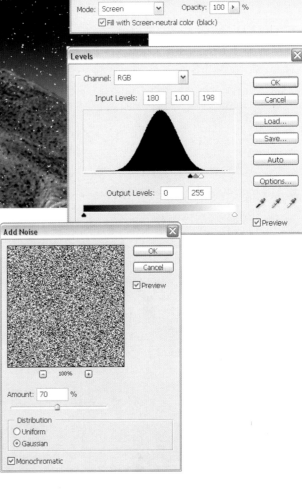

7 One of the problems with the *Gradient* tool, and traditional gradient filters for cameras, is that the gradient darkens any element within the area being darkened—in this case, the mountain. To remove the gradient from the central mountain, use the layer mask attached to the gradient layer and paint out the mountain. Finally, change the blending mode of the gradient layer to *Multiply*. We now have a night sky.

8 We can complete the lunar effect by adding some stars. Press Shift + Ctrl (Cmd) + N to open the *New Layer* dialog, and use the settings shown here to create a new layer in *Screen* mode. Apply the *Noise* filter with the settings shown, followed by the *Gaussian Blur* filter at a one-pixel radius. Then apply a *Levels* adjustment as shown in the *Levels* dialog. The result should be a star-filled layer. If desired, the density of the stars can be reduced by repeating the *Gaussian Blur* and *Levels* stages more than once.

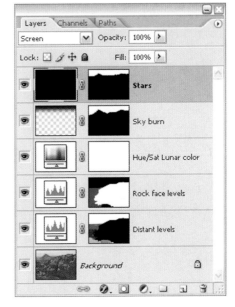

9 At the moment there are stars over the landscape that need to be hidden using the layer mask. Use a black brush to paint out the unwanted stars, and then use the *Lasso* tool to select the rest of the stars and fill this selection in to hide them.

VICTORIAN SEPIA TONING

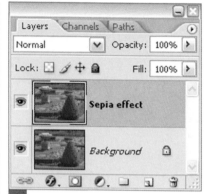

2 Start by dragging the background layer to the *Create a new layer* button at the bottom of the *Layers* palette to duplicate it. We want to preserve the original for later enhancement. Rename the new layer "Sepia effect."

1 I am using a picture of a formal garden, typical of the photographs of the period. However, this effect can be applied to any picture in the same way. Don't worry about adjusting the tonal values at this stage—we will do this after the aging effect has been applied.

Victorian photographs hold a special appeal. Whether it is nostalgia for a bygone era, or simply the particular visual qualities of the Victorian photographic style, old prints with their sepia-brown tones and faded borders are always popular.

With Photoshop at our disposal, emulating the characteristics of a Victorian photograph on modern digital pictures is not difficult. This project will take you through the various steps required to recreate the mood of an old Victorian print.

3 Press Ctrl (Cmd) + U on your keyboard to open the *Hue/Saturation* dialog. Tick in the *Colorize* check-box to activate it. This allows us to apply color toning to the entire image while retaining the tonal values. Set the *Hue* slider to 20 and the *Saturation* to 25, then press the *Enter* key.

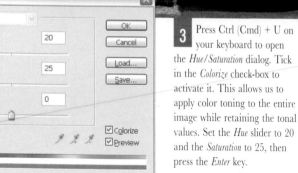

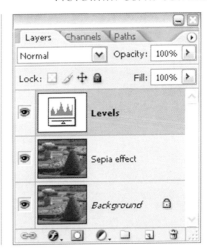

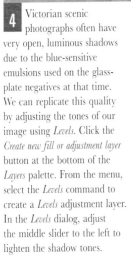

4 Victorian scenic photographs often have very open, luminous shadows due to the blue-sensitive emulsions used on the glass-plate negatives at that time. We can replicate this quality by adjusting the tones of our image using *Levels*. Click the *Create new fill or adjustment layer* button at the bottom of the *Layers* palette. From the menu, select the *Levels* command to create a *Levels* adjustment layer. In the *Levels* dialog, adjust the middle slider to the left to lighten the shadow tones.

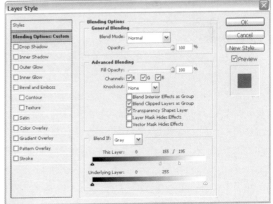

5 Another characteristic of Victorian prints is that they are often faded around the edges. To produce this effect, simply create a new layer above the others and name it "Edge fade." Now, with a very large soft brush (300 pixels, in this case), and with white as the foreground color, paint around the edges of the image. Don't try to be exact with the lines since real fading isn't usually even. Also, apply a little more white in the corners since they usually fade the most. Reduce the *Opacity* of the edge fade to around 60% so some of the image shows through.

6 As a final enhancement, we can use the *Layer Styles* dialog to selectively hide some of our sepia layer, allowing a little of the original color from the background layer to show through the toning. Double-click the sepia layer and adjust the *This layer* white slider as shown in the dialog. Alt (Opt) + click the slider to split it into two for a subtle transition between the tones.

HAND COLORING

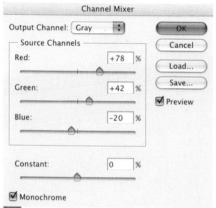

1 Hand coloring is best applied to strong compositions like this flower picture. Simple shapes, similar tones and open detail can be colored much more easily than very complex shapes with a lot of fussy detail.

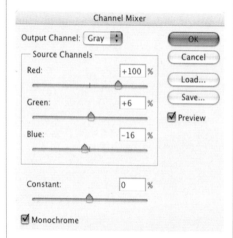

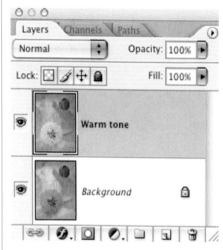

Made popular when true color photography was yet to be invented, hand coloring is the term given to the process of adding color to a black-and-white print. Various media can be used, but the most popular modern method is to use photo-quality, water-based dyes. Unfortunately, as with many of the traditional techniques, it takes a great deal of artistic skill to produce good-quality results. However, by using digital imaging, it is possible to produce very good hand-colored images with only a little practice—and of course mistakes can be remedied quite easily.

In this project you will learn the techniques required to simulate traditional hand-colored results on any picture you choose.

2 If you are starting with a color image, the first step is to convert it to black and white. Although it may be tempting simply to use the *Desaturate* command, this rarely produces the best monotone conversion. First duplicate the background layer and then use the *Channel Mixer* (see the "Flipping an Image" project on pages 172–175 for more on using the *Channel Mixer*) to convert the new image layer to black and white. Name this layer "Warm tone."

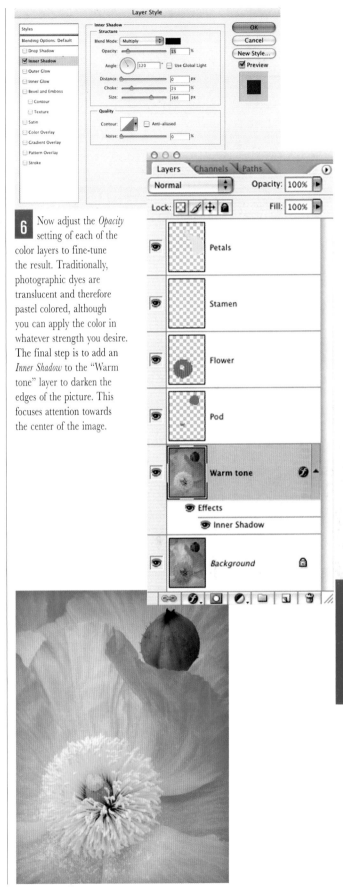

4 To add color to the image, create a new layer above the sepia layer and name it. Here I have named it "Pod" since I will be coloring the seed pod first. Change the blending mode of this layer to *Color*. Now paint on this layer over the desired area of the image with a colored brush. Here I've used a rich green color. Use the brush in normal mode at 100% *Opacity*. We will adjust the layer opacity later to reduce the saturation of the colors.

6 Now adjust the *Opacity* setting of each of the color layers to fine-tune the result. Traditionally, photographic dyes are translucent and therefore pastel colored, although you can apply the color in whatever strength you desire. The final step is to add an *Inner Shadow* to the "Warm tone" layer to darken the edges of the picture. This focuses attention towards the center of the image.

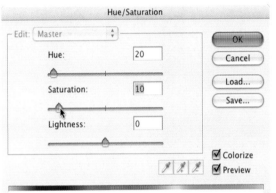

3 Traditionally, photographic prints are given a sepia tone before being colored, to warm up any black-and-white areas. This is not essential for digital hand coloring, but it does produce a pleasing result. Press Ctrl (Cmd) + U to open the *Hue/Saturation* dialog. Click the *Colorize* check-box to activate it, then set the *Hue* to 20 and the *Saturation* to 15 for a subtle effect.

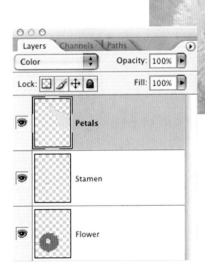

5 Repeat Step 4 for the other elements of the image you wish to hand color. Color each layer separately for greater flexibility, and so that individual changes can be made.

GRAPHIC COLOR AND GRAIN

One popular technique among art photographers is to create very graphic images using grainy and soft-focus effects. In the past this was achieved using the fastest possible color film and some form of soft-focus filtration, in the manner of David Hamilton and Sarah Moon; or by re-photographing a small area of a normal transparency using fast film and a slide copier.

This copying process emphasized the grainy quality of the photograph and reduced the definition of the image. By accentuating the film contrast during development of the duplicates, the results often appeared dramatic and unnatural.

This type of graphic effect is now much simpler to produce using Photoshop, with the added bonus that it is quicker and easier to control the process digitally. One great advantage of this technique is that the original image doesn't need to be a great shot, since the point is to find a new, exciting composition from within the original scene. This is a great way to make use of otherwise uninteresting pictures. So, switch your mind into surreal mode and use the following project as a basis for your own creative exploration.

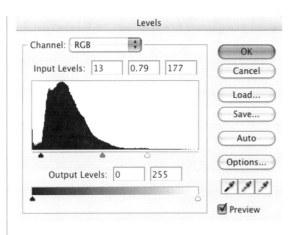

1 Use an image with good colors and a strong graphic arrangement of subject matter. The first step is to use the *Crop* tool, so press C on the keyboard to isolate the area of interest, as shown in this picture of poppies in a grassy field. Since the *Crop* tool darkens the image outside the region to be cropped, it is very easy to experiment with finding a good composition. Since the background layer is less flexible than a normal layer, I find it useful to convert it at the start of a project. Do this by double-clicking the background layer. Type a name in the resulting dialog box and press *Enter*.

2 Since the image is only a small part of the original, it is necessary to resize it using the *Image Size* command from the *Image* menu. Make sure the *Resample Image* and *Constrain Proportions* check-boxes are selected and enter new values for the height and resolution as desired. In this case the image was resized from a height of 2" (5cm) to 8" (20cm) and the resolution set to 300 dpi. Once the image is at the required size, use the *Levels* command to boost the contrast. This will help to give the image a more graphic quality.

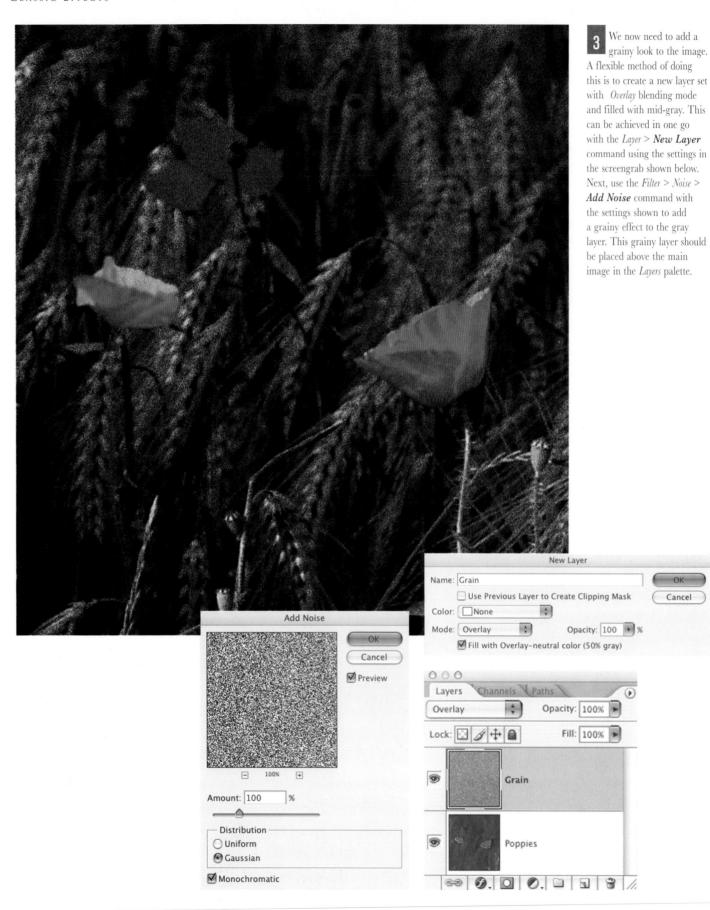

3 We now need to add a grainy look to the image. A flexible method of doing this is to create a new layer set with *Overlay* blending mode and filled with mid-gray. This can be achieved in one go with the *Layer* > **New Layer** command using the settings in the screengrab shown below. Next, use the *Filter* > *Noise* > **Add Noise** command with the settings shown to add a grainy effect to the gray layer. This grainy layer should be placed above the main image in the *Layers* palette.

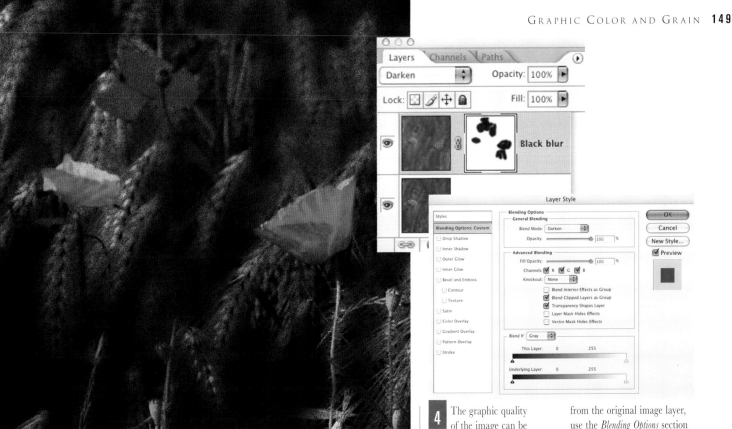

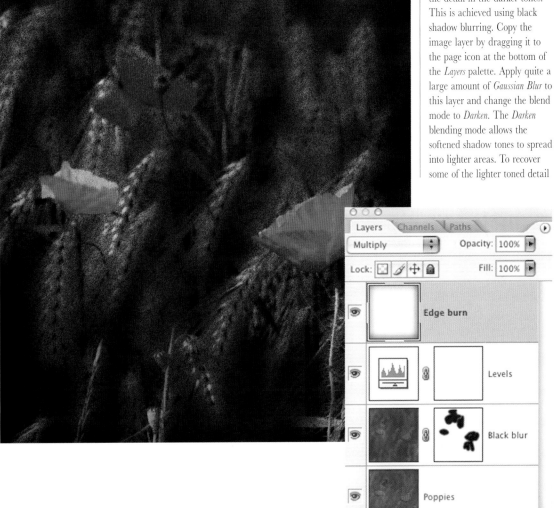

4 The graphic quality of the image can be improved by removing some of the detail in the darker tones. This is achieved using black shadow blurring. Copy the image layer by dragging it to the page icon at the bottom of the *Layers* palette. Apply quite a large amount of *Gaussian Blur* to this layer and change the blend mode to *Darken*. The *Darken* blending mode allows the softened shadow tones to spread into lighter areas. To recover some of the lighter toned detail from the original image layer, use the *Blending Options* section of the *Layer Style* dialog (double-click the layer to open the *Layer Style* dialog) for the blur layer. Move the white slider below the *This Layer* tone scale to expose the tones from the lower layer. Split the slider by Alt (Opt) + clicking it to smooth the transition of the tones. As shown in the layers screengrab, I have used a layer mask on the blur layer to control where the effect is allowed to act, since some areas became too dark.

5 The final image required minor tonal adjustments using a *Levels* adjustment layer. I also like to use edge darkening on many of my images to focus attention into the image. Use a new layer in *Multiply* mode and the *Gradient* tool to create the graduated edges. These can be further softened using *Gaussian blur*, and the opacity of the layer reduced to control the edge burning.

GRADUATED FILTERS

1 Here we have the classic problem of an overly bright sky and a dark evening landscape. This requires the use of a digital graduated filter.

Graduated filters usually have a light-to-dark tint and are used in front of the camera lens to lower the tonal values of one part of the scene. The usual application of graduated filters in traditional photography is to darken a bright sky, so that the contrast between the sky and landscape is more acceptable. Graduated filters can be either neutral in tone, or have a color tint for use with color pictures. The limitation of the camera filter is that the gradient is linear. This is often noticeable when the foreground rises above the horizon; for example, when a tree overlaps the sky, the treetop is darkened by the filter while the trunk remains unnaturally light.

The digital equivalent of a graduated filter is to apply the Gradient tool on a new blank layer above the main image. The advantage of the digital version is that you can make infinite adjustments to refine the shape of the gradient layer by using the Gradient tool in Multiply mode. This allows you to make the graduated effect fit the shape of the sky much more effectively. Also, by changing the blending mode of the graduated layer you can experiment with different results.

2 Create a new blank layer above the main image. Click on the *Gradient* tool, and in the *Options* bar click the gradient and choose the *Foreground to Transparent* gradient. Next, set the mode to *Multiply*. Leave the *Opacity* at 100%. Click the mouse at the top of the sky and drag down as far as necessary. Hold the Shift key down so the gradient is straight.

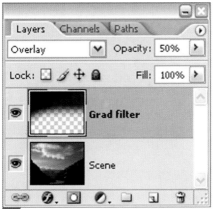

3 If necessary, continue to apply more gradients at different angles to build up the final effect. Here the sky was brighter at the left of the image, so I applied a second gradient at an angle to correct this. Next I changed the blending mode to *Overlay* and reduced the *Opacity* to 50%. The final gradient layer is shown above.

4 It is very common for photographers to use warm filters on the camera, and Photoshop has the same facility built in. I added a new Photo filter adjustment layer and selected the *Warm Filter (85)* at 50% to add a pleasant warm tone to the whole image.

DEPTH OF FIELD

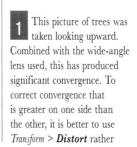

Depth of field is traditionally defined as that part of a photograph which is acceptably sharp to the human eye. This is primarily controlled by the aperture used when making the exposure for the picture. Since depth of field is an optical effect that creates a specific region of sharpness, the only control the traditional photographer had was his choice of aperture. This restriction does not apply in the world of digital imaging, and a more creative use of sharpness and blur effects can be employed to tantalize our normal visual perception.

This project will show you the basic method for producing unusual digital depth of field, giving you the skills necessary to explore this topic more thoroughly on your own images.

1 This picture of trees was taken looking upward. Combined with the wide-angle lens used, this has produced significant convergence. To correct convergence that is greater on one side than the other, it is better to use *Transform > **Distort*** rather than *Transform > **Perspective***. The latter command only allows symmetrical correction, and we need different corrections to be made to the trees on each side. Start by converting the background layer into a normal layer by double-clicking its thumbnail, then name it "Trees." Next, access the *Transform > **Distort*** command on the *Edit* menu and remove the convergence by dragging the top-corner handles.

2 To create the depth-of-field effect, we need to use feathered selections and the *Lens Blur* filter. The *Lens Blur* filter has various settings that enable you to control the blur effect. The simplest depth-of-field effect is to have a narrow section in the middle distance of the scene sharp, and the rest out of focus. To do this, use the *Rectangular Marquee* tool and draw three selections, one at each side of the image and one in the middle, to define the areas you want blurred. Hold the Shift key down after the first rectangle is drawn to allow the other two to be added. Switch to *Quick Mask* mode by pressing Q on your keyboard. Note that the center rectangle stops short of the bottom of the image to keep that area sharp.

3 Apply some *Gaussian Blur* to the selection to soften the edges, producing a graduated change of sharpness for the depth of field. Press Q to return to a normal selection and use the *Select > Save Selection* command to store the selection in a new *Alpha* channel named "Narrow DoF." Press Ctrl (Cmd) + D to deselect the selection.

4 Copy the main image layer to a new layer named "Narrow DoF." Open the *Blur > **Lens Blur*** filter dialog. In the *Depth Map* section, choose the saved "Narrow DoF" selection from the *Source* drop-down list; this will determine which parts of the image are blurred. The

Radius setting controls the amount of blurring to simulate different camera apertures, and the *Noise* setting adds digital noise to simulate film grain in the blurred areas which would otherwise look unnaturally smooth. All the settings used for this version of the image are shown in the dialog screengrab.

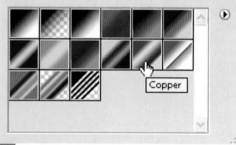

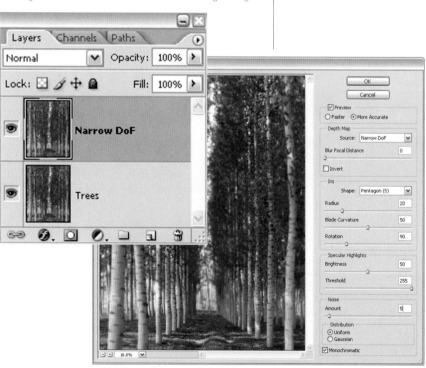

5 More creative depth-of-field effects can be produced by using more unusual selections. Make a new copy of the original image layer and rename it. To make the selection for the version shown here, first enter *Quick Mask* mode by pressing Q on your keyboard. Click on the *Gradient tool* button in the toolbox and then choose the *Copper* gradient from the *Options* bar. Now apply the *Copper* gradient across the image from left to right. Press Q to exit *Quick Mask* and convert to a normal selection then save it using the *Select > **Save Selection*** command. I named the saved selection "Fun DoF." Now deselect by pressing Ctrl (Cmd) + D.

6 Open the *Lens > Blur* filter dialog as before, and choose the "Fun DoF" saved selection in the *Source* box. Adjust the other settings as desired and click *OK*. The result is much more unusual with subtle changes of focus in different parts of the image. This is the result of the more complex *Alpha* channel mask, shown in the screengrab, used as the source for the *Lens Blur* filter.

7 The depth-of-field effect produced by the *Lens Blur* filter can be further refined using a layer mask on the blurred layer. With the unfiltered original image layer below, you can paint out areas of the blurred layer to reveal sharp details from the original image, making the picture even more arresting.

MOVEMENT

When photographing landscape subjects, movement in the scene can either be a useful or a distinctly undesirable occurrence. Most of the time it is unwanted, but it has been used creatively by some notable photographers to produce distinctive images. Movement in a photograph is seen as blurring of subject details. The amount of blur indicates the level of movement present; small or slow movement produces small amounts of blur. The blurring from subject movement is also dependent on the shutter speed used when exposing the picture.

Even slow movement can be made to record with lots of blur if the shutter time is sufficiently long. Conversely, lots of subject movement can be made to record with less blur by using a short or fast shutter time.

These traditional methods of controlling blur due to movement can be replicated digitally in Photoshop using the various blur filters. This project shows the methods of applying blur filters to simulate the movement of tree branches. The techniques used here can be applied to any image.

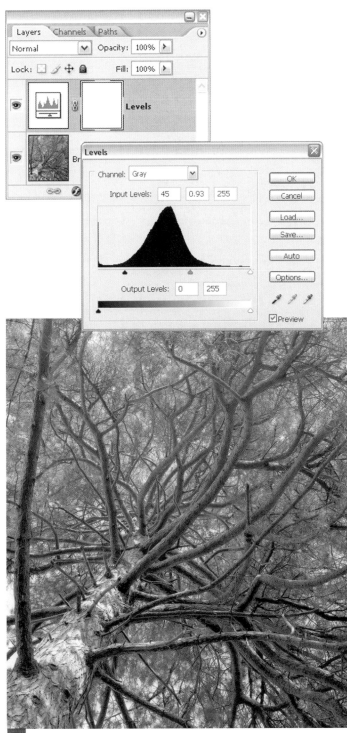

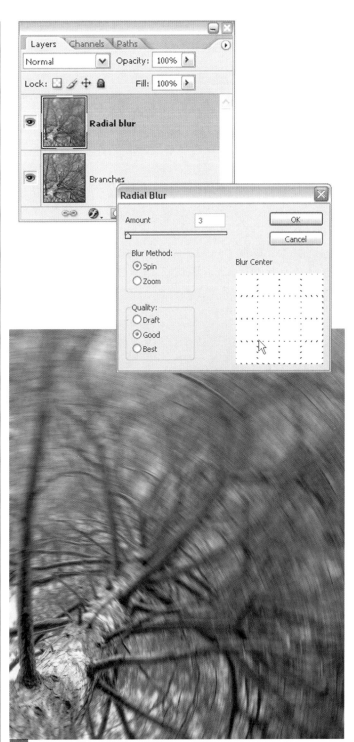

1 Starting with a subject that is naturally affected by movement allows you to produce either relatively natural effects or, as here, rather more unusual results. The first task is to correct the contrast of the image using a *Levels* adjustment layer. When you are happy with the contrast, merge the layers.

2 Create a copy of the main image layer by dragging it to the *Create a new layer* button on the *Layers* palette. Now apply the *Blur > **Radial Blur*** filter using settings adequate for your image. For movement that naturally creates an arc—as with these tree branches, where the tops will move more than the lower parts—set the *Blur Method* to *Spin*. You can also adjust the center of rotation for the filter by dragging in the *Blur Center* box. In this image I have placed the blur center to coincide with the main trunk of the tree. In this way the blur is rotating more naturally around the tree's axis.

3 There are several ways to make the layers interact with each other using blending modes, but since in this scene we want to combine sharp and blurred areas of the picture, the easiest method is to use a layer mask. Add a layer mask to the "Radial blur" layer and use the black brush to paint on the layer mask. In this case I am revealing several of the unfiltered, thicker tree branches since they would not naturally move much. The great thing about layer masks is the ability to correct mistakes as you work, or to simply paint with a white brush if you change your mind.

Tip

It is very easy to apply blur to a sharp image to simulate movement, but virtually impossible to work the other way. Therefore, when you photograph scenes on which you may want to experiment with digital movement effects, try and achieve the sharpest image possible using good depth of field and a fast shutter speed.

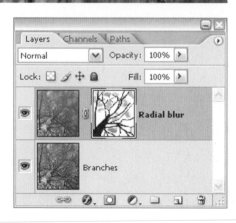

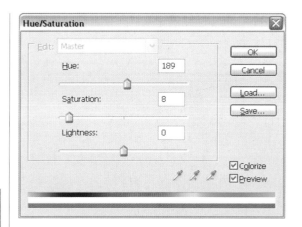

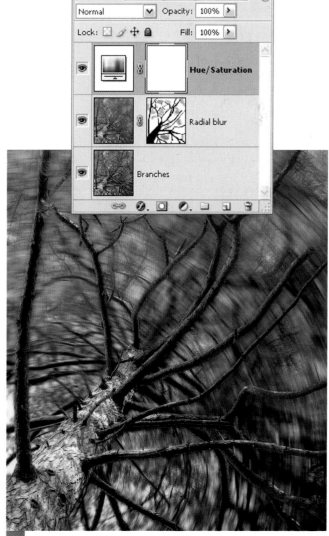

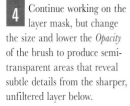

4 Continue working on the layer mask, but change the size and lower the *Opacity* of the brush to produce semi-transparent areas that reveal subtle details from the sharper, unfiltered layer below.

5 Grayscale images such as this often benefit from the addition of digital toning. The toning method used here is to convert the image to *RGB* mode and then add a *Hue/* *Saturation* adjustment layer with the *Colorize* option box checked. Adjust the *Hue* slider to obtain the desired color and then alter the *Saturation* slider to determine the depth of color.

FISHEYE LENS EFFECT

Fisheye lenses, especially those in the 35mm format, produce intriguing images due to the massive distortion of the subject. Unfortunately, such extreme lenses tend to be very expensive. As with many other visual effects, it is possible to simulate the look of a fisheye picture using the tools available in Photoshop. This project will show you how easy it is, using only a single filter, to create your own brand of fisheye images.

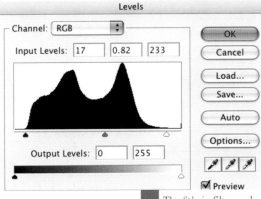

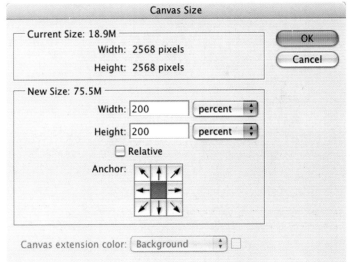

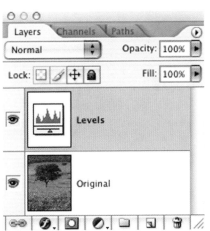

1 The *Spherize* filter used to produce the effect in this project works best on a square image, so the first step is to crop your picture to a square shape. The filter also works well when the main subject is in or near the middle of the frame, as in this simple picture. As usual, start by correcting any contrast and color problems using a *Levels* adjustment layer. Now double-click the background layer to convert it to a normal layer and name it.

2 The *Crop* tool can be used with the modifier keys Shift and Alt (Opt) to control how it draws the crop boundaries. Pressing and holding the Shift key while dragging the mouse makes a square with its top-left corner at the start of the drag. Pressing and holding both the Shift and Alt (Opt) keys while dragging creates a square with its center at the start of the drag. This is the best method for this project since it allows you to specify the exact center of the square. Crop your image as described.

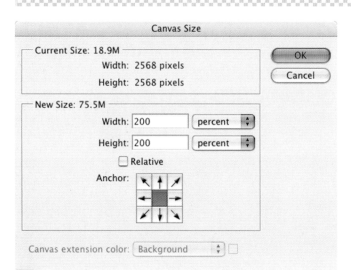

3 The *Spherize* filter affects a circle within the boundaries of the image, so the corners of the picture are not affected by the filter. Since we want to spherize the entire image it is necessary to increase the size of the canvas so our image is within the effective circle of the filter. Also, each application of the filter will increase the image size, so we need to allow room for this expansion. Select the *Image > **Canvas Size*** command and double the size of the canvas in the *Canvas Size* dialog. The easiest way to do this is to select *Percent* from the drop-down list for *Width* and *Height* and enter 200 for each dimension.

4 Now apply the *Distort > **Spherize*** filter with the *Amount* set to 100% and mode to *Normal*. As you can see, one application of the filter produces an effect like barrel distortion. Note that the filter also increases the actual image size.

5 We want the image to have the appearance of a complete 180° fisheye-lens effect, so it is necessary to apply the filter several times. To do this, press Ctrl (Cmd) + F on your keyboard a further two or three times, or until the image becomes a circle, as shown. We now have our fisheye image.

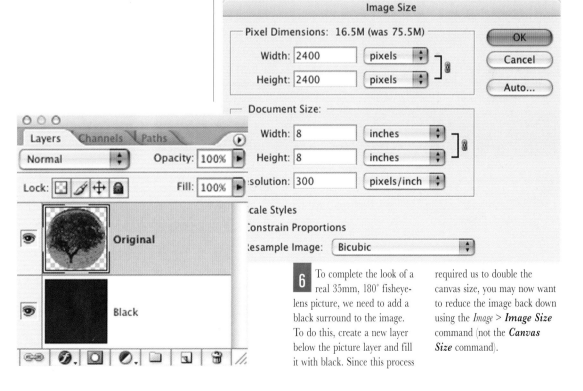

6 To complete the look of a real 35mm, 180° fisheye-lens picture, we need to add a black surround to the image. To do this, create a new layer below the picture layer and fill it with black. Since this process required us to double the canvas size, you may now want to reduce the image back down using the *Image* > **Image Size** command (not the **Canvas Size** command).

Lens Flare

Whenever there is a bright source of light in the picture, or just outside the picture area, it often causes internal reflections in the lens of the camera. These reflections may manifest themselves as rings in the picture that are the same shape as the aperture. They are most prominent in the shadow areas of the image since they are usually light in tone.

It would be quite difficult to create these flare effects manually, but fortunately Photoshop has a dedicated Lens Flare filter that makes it easy to apply the effect to any image. This project will show you how easy it is to use this filter to give an evocative mood to an otherwise straightforward picture.

1 Lens flare effects are seen most in the shadow areas of the image since they are reflections of a bright light source. Therefore, choose an image with large areas of shadow, like this picture of stones from an ancient stone circle monument. Use a *Levels* adjustment layer to darken the shadow values as much as possible without losing essential details.

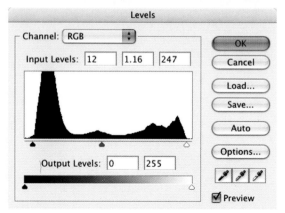

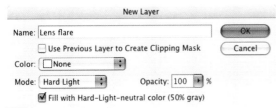

2 The *Lens Flare* filter needs a filled layer to work on, so press Shift + Ctrl (Cmd) + N on your keyboard to open the *New Layer* dialog. Use the settings shown here,

and remember to click the *Fill* checkbox. Press *Enter* to create the new layer. If necessary, drag the new layer to the top of the layers stack in the *Layers* palette.

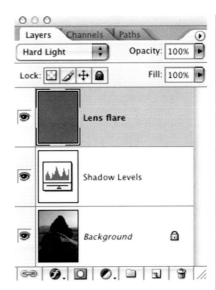

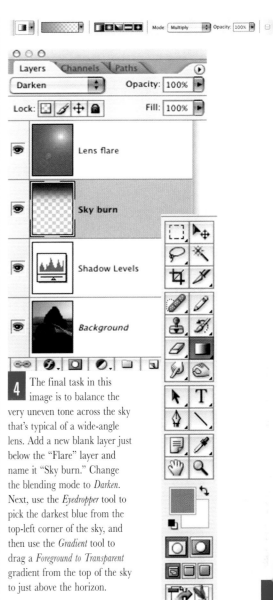

4 The final task in this image is to balance the very uneven tone across the sky that's typical of a wide-angle lens. Add a new blank layer just below the "Flare" layer and name it "Sky burn." Change the blending mode to *Darken*. Next, use the *Eyedropper* tool to pick the darkest blue from the top-left corner of the sky, and then use the *Gradient* tool to drag a *Foreground to Transparent* gradient from the top of the sky to just above the horizon.

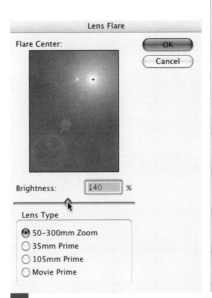

3 Use the *Filter > Render > Lens Flare* command to open the filter dialog. With your mouse, drag the crosshairs in the *Flare Center* preview area to roughly position the source of the flare and control the angle and direction of the flare itself. For this image, the crosshairs represent the location of the sun in the sky, which is obviously to the right of the picture, and which I want to position to be peeking out from behind the right edge

of the stones. The *Brightness* percentage slider controls the strength of the flare. The *Lens Type* is used to change the look of the flare rings—experiment with it until you find a style that suits your image. Apply the filter and, if necessary, use the *Move* tool on the flare layer to fine-tune the position of the flare, and use the *Edit > Transform* tools to adjust the scale and rotation.

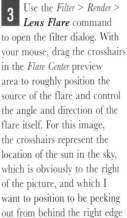

BLACK-SHADOW SOFT FOCUS

An unusual darkroom technique often applied to traditional black-and-white prints is known as black-shadow soft focus. This is created by placing some form of diffuser (a black nylon stocking was traditionally used) under the enlarger lens during the print exposure. This creates a dark blur around the shadows of the image, effectively spreading them into nearby lighter tones. This is the opposite of the more usual soft-focus effect applied when taking the photograph, which adds a glow to the light tones in the image.

1 Prepare your landscape image by correcting any contrast and color problems using *Levels* adjustments. Then convert the background into a normal layer by double-clicking on the thumbnail in the *Layers* palette and renaming the layer.

2 Duplicate the original layer by dragging it to the *Create a new layer* button at the bottom of the *Layers* palette. Rename this layer "Shadow blur." Now use the *Filter > Blur > Gaussian Blur* filter to apply a small amount of diffusion to this layer. This will blur the entire image.

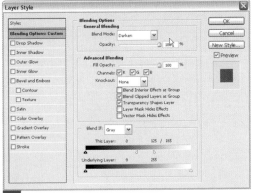

3 Double-click the "shadow blur" thumbnail in the *Layers* palette to open the *Layer Style* dialog. Change the blending mode to *Darken* and adjust the white slider on the *This Layer* tone scale as shown. Adjusting this slider removes the lighter tones from the blurred layer, leaving only the shadow tones.

4 Another favorite technique of darkroom printers is to darken the edges of the image to draw attention to the center of the print. We can create the same effect using the *Inner Glow* layer style. Once you are happy with the blur effect, use the *Layer Palette* menu and apply the *Merge Visible* command. Do not use the *Flatten Image* command since layer styles do not work on the background layer. Now click the *Add a layer style* button on the palette and select the *Inner Glow* style from the menu. To place quite a dark edge around the image, as I have done, use similar settings to those shown in the dialog and remember to change the color to black.

COLOR TO MONOCHROME

Traditional film-based photography has always been defined in terms of color or black-and-white images. The type of image you wanted was determined by the type of film you loaded into your camera. For the digital photographer, or those using a scanner, the choice of whether to produce a black-and-white or color picture can be left until you want to make a print. When using a digital camera, always record the image as a RAW file in full color, because, as this project will show, you have at your disposal a very flexible method of converting a color image into black and white using Adobe Photoshop. This method is so flexible that you can, if you wish, use it to emulate the style of other black-and-white photographers.

In this project we shall attempt to recreate the style of one of the most famous exponents of black-and-white photography, Ansel Adams. The prints of Ansel Adams are characterized by strong, scenic contrasts. Adams also used dramatic filtration to produce high-impact skies, and many of his pictures contain graphic foreground interest with mountains in the distance. This is the look we shall pursue here.

1 This picture has the typical compositional elements of an Ansel Adams landscape: a strong foreground leading to distant mountains. Although not essential for this technique, I prefer to correct any tone and contrast issues on the color image using a *Levels* adjustment layer before proceeding to the monochrome conversion stage. You will find that if the original color image has correct contrast, it makes it easier to assess the channels, as described next.

2 To help you decide on the type of monochrome image you want in terms of overall contrast and tonal relationships, examine each of the individual color channels in the image using the *Channels* palette. Open the *Channels* palette and click on the *Red*, *Green*, and *Blue* channels individually to examine the tones of each grayscale channel. The images above show the results of the *Red*, *Green* and *Blue* channels, from left to right. Since we want to emulate Ansel Adams' style, we need the channel that shows the most dramatic tonal difference between the yellow flowers and the rest of the scene, and, if possible, a darkened sky. The *Red* channel offers the best result, and this will be used later in the *Channel Mixer* dialog.

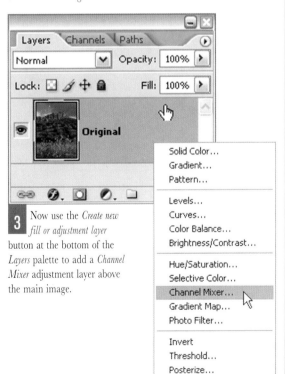

3 Now use the *Create new fill or adjustment layer* button at the bottom of the *Layers* palette to add a *Channel Mixer* adjustment layer above the main image.

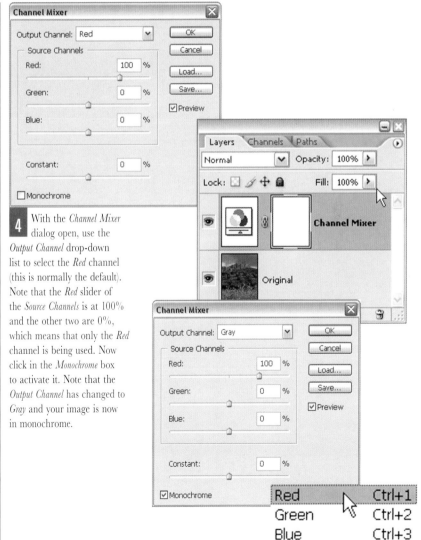

4 With the *Channel Mixer* dialog open, use the *Output Channel* drop-down list to select the *Red* channel (this is normally the default). Note that the *Red* slider of the *Source Channels* is at 100% and the other two are 0%, which means that only the *Red* channel is being used. Now click in the *Monochrome* box to activate it. Note that the *Output Channel* has changed to *Gray* and your image is now in monochrome.

5 Now the fun can really begin. By adjusting the *Red*, *Green*, and *Blue* sliders under *Source Channels*, we can adjust the amount of information each color channel will contribute to our final converted image. The permutations are endless, so use your judgment to determine the required settings. The result shown here is based on our emulation of a landscape in the style of Ansel Adams.

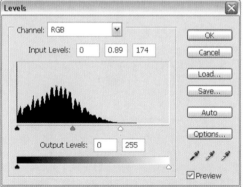

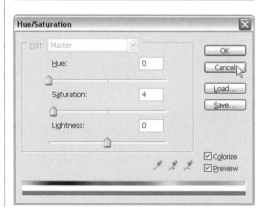

6 The *Channel Mixer* conversion is great, but you may need to make further tonal adjustments to get the image just right. To make this more like an Ansel Adams image, we need to darken the sky for added drama and increase the contrast of the rocky mountain. Select each area in turn and add a *Levels* adjustment layer based on the selection to localize the effect where needed. Finally, to give it the look of an early print, add a *Hue/Saturation* adjustment layer with the *Colorize* check-box ticked and add a sepia tone.

THE CHANNEL MIXER DIALOG

Let's sidetrack for a moment to examine what happens to the actual tones of an image when we adjust the *Red*, *Green*, and *Blue* sliders in the *Channel Mixer* dialog. To avoid tonal distortions and posterization, it is recommended that the total of the three slider values adds up to 100%. We can see why using the *Channel Mixer* dialog and the expanded histogram window showing how the tones of the image are being affected by changes to the settings in the dialog box.

A shows the *Channel Mixer* dialog with its starting values—note only the *Red* slider is used, and the resulting *Histogram* window of the landscape image used in this project. The histogram shows graphically how the tonal distribution will be affected if this *Channel Mixer* conversion is applied.

Now let's start by increasing only the *Red* slider to 118% (**B**) without changing the other two colors. The accompanying *Histogram* now shows gaps, meaning that tones are being lost. Note also that the right edge of the *Histogram* shows some of the lightest tones being pushed into pure white, thus losing subtle detail (the overall image contrast has increased).

If we now adjust the *Blue* slider to -18% (**C**) to compensate for the increased *Red*, we see that the Histogram is again complete, indicating there are no lost tones. Also, the lightest tones are now back on the graph. This shows clearly why it is important that these three values add up to 100%.

The *Constant* slider is used to lighten or darken all the tones equally, and is used for final adjustment of the image brightness if needed. We can see this in changes to our Histogram. **D** is the default *Histogram* and **F** is the result of setting the *Constant* value to 15% (**E** shows the *Channel Mixer* settings for this). Note that the graph in **F** has moved to the right, but that the general shape is almost the same as the graph in **D**, indicating that all the tones have increased by an equal amount, resulting in a lighter image.

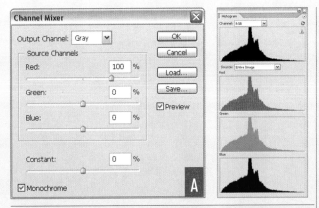

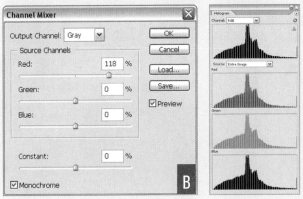

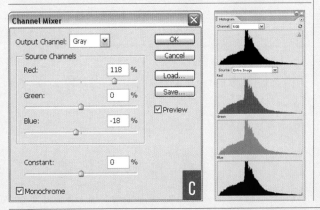

Tip

You may be tempted simply to copy one of the color channels to use as your converted monochrome image. This is a bad idea, as these two *Histograms* show. As you can see, the *Histogram* of a copy of only the *Red channel* for this landscape shows gaps in the graph. These gaps represent the absence of tones, caused by not using the detail present in the *Green* and *Blue* channels. This results in less smoothness in the image tones and mild posterization. The second Histogram is of the image converted using the *Channel Mixer* method. Note that this *Histogram* has no gaps, showing there is no loss of tonal values after conversion.

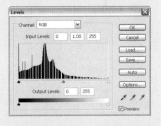

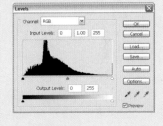

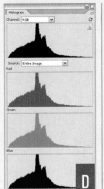

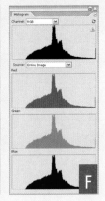

FLIPPING AN IMAGE

Perfect symmetry is rarely found in nature and certainly not in landscape scenes. However, symmetry is a fascinating aspect of visual composition that can be used to produce unusual pictures or to strengthen the mood of a scene.

The easiest way to create symmetry in Photoshop is to simply use Transform > Flip Horizontal on a duplicate layer of the main image, then double the canvas width and move the images until they are side by side. However, the perfect symmetry that results can produce rather a crude effect when applied to a landscape picture. With the addition of the extra few steps shown in this project, you can turn that crude effect into a subtle and intriguing version of the original image.

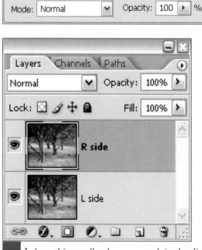

1 I chose this woodland scene because of its quiet mood and beautifully soft light. Adding symmetry to the image will help to emphasize this atmosphere. Start by double-clicking the background layer, and, in the dialog that opens, name the layer and click *OK*. This converts it to a normal layer. Duplicate this layer by dragging it to the *Create a new layer button* on the *Layers* palette, and then rename it.

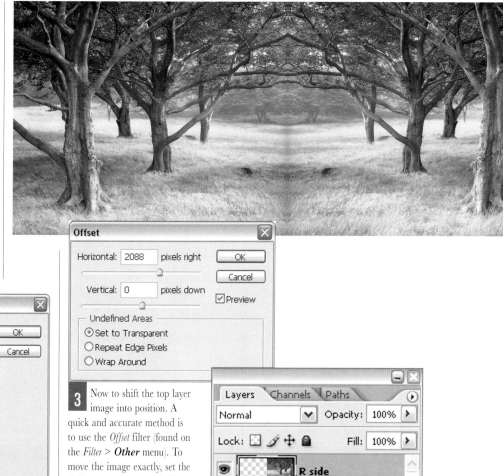

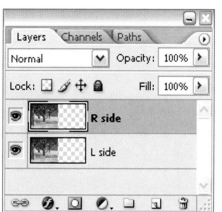

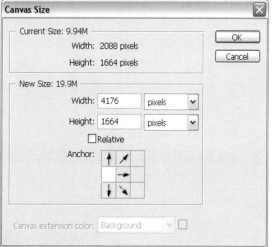

2 Use the *Canvas Size* command from the *Image* menu to double the width of the canvas. Be sure to set the *Anchor* point to the left side as shown in the dialog above. Make the top layer active and apply *Transform > **Flip Horizontal*** from the *Edit* menu.

3 Now to shift the top layer image into position. A quick and accurate method is to use the *Offset* filter (found on the *Filter > **Other*** menu). To move the image exactly, set the *Horizontal pixel* value to half the canvas width in pixels, and set the *Vertical* value to zero.

4 We are now ready to determine the best center line for the image—in this instance it is the faint tree in the distance. With the top layer active, drag a rectangular selection from the right side of the image until the left edge cuts through the distant tree. With the selection active, add a layer mask to the top layer using the *Reveal Selection* option.

5 Now use the *Move* tool to position the top layer image so that the distant tree creates a mirror image with the same tree on the bottom layer. Use the arrow direction keys to fine-tune the position in one-pixel steps. Next, use the *Crop* tool to remove unwanted parts of the canvas. Here the image is cropped so the trees form a frame, increasing the natural tunnel effect.

6 We now have the basic, but crude, mirror effect of flipping the image. Now use the *Clone Stamp* tool to disguise that horrible center line symmetry, producing a more natural effect. Clone parts of the image that are sympathetic in tone to the areas to be covered. Here the foliage has been replaced, but the tree branch joins are retained to form a series of "natural" arches. When ready the image layers can be flattened to reduce the file size.

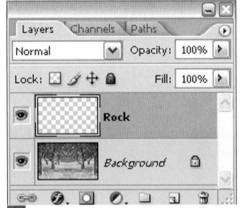

7 To add more interest to the scene, and to give the symmetrical effect some subtlety, we can add one of the digital rocks created in an earlier project (see pages 32–33). Since the image is in *Grayscale* mode, and we will be toning it later, convert it to color using the *Image > Mode* > **RGB Color** command. Open a previously created rock file and copy the rock to the woodland scene by dragging its image from one window to the other—this will place it on a new layer. It may be necessary to isolate the rock by removing any white background.

8 Create a new layer set and drag the "Rock" layer into it. Resize the rock image using *Transform > **Scale*** and convert it to monochrome using the *Channel Mixer*.

10 To add realism, we need to make the rock appear to sit in the grass, so the grass needs to overlap the bottom edge of the rock. Add a layer mask to the "Rock" layer and use a soft brush to hide the bottom of the rock. Slightly reduce the overall sharpness of the rock using a very small amount of *Gaussian Blur*.

9 Load the "Rock" layer transparency as a selection by Ctrl (Cmd) + clicking on the "Rock" layer. With this selection active, add a *Levels* adjustment layer to the "Rock" layer set and adjust the contrast of the rock to match the rest of the scene.

11 To complete the realism, add a *Drop Shadow* layer style to the "Rock" layer to place a faint, soft shadow in front of the rock. The settings are shown in the dialog box above left. Finally, above all the other layers, add a *Hue/ Saturation* adjustment layer with the *Colorize* box checked to give tone to the entire image.

MAKING A PANORAMA

Panoramas first became popular when Victorian photographers traveling the world wanted to capture the grandeur of the wild places they were discovering. Because lens formats were in their relative infancy, especially wide-angle designs, and extreme wide-angle lenses were not available, special panoramic cameras were invented. These cameras captured a full 180-degree scene in one image, producing the long, horizontal photograph now classically associated with a panoramic view.

People are still enthusiastic about panoramic images and they are as popular as ever. Fortunately, with Photoshop it is now easier than ever to produce your own panoramic views. This project will show you, by using Photoshop's built-in Photomerge command, how easy it is to combine several images into a panorama, transforming an average scene into something much more interesting.

1 I made six different, portrait-format images, all with the lens focused at the same distance using the same exposure. This minimizes image distortion and tone changes. Place all the images in a new folder on your computer and name them sequentially—e.g. "image1.tif," "image2.tif," etc. Use *Levels* to make the image contrast and the color balance the same for all of the images.

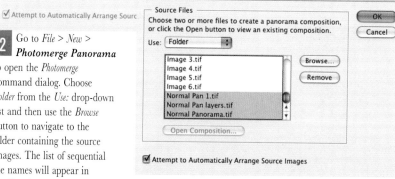

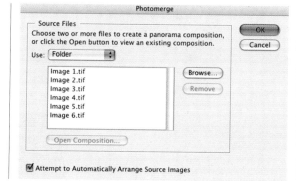

2 Go to *File > New >*
Photomerge Panorama
to open the *Photomerge*
command dialog. Choose
Folder from the *Use:* drop-down
list and then use the *Browse*
button to navigate to the
folder containing the source
images. The list of sequential
file names will appear in
the file window. If there are
any files in the list that are
not part of your panorama,
highlight them and use the
Remove button to clear them
from the list. Click the *OK*
button when the list is ready.

4 If there are any images
that have not been
stitched, drag them into the
correct position from the top
panel onto the preview and
align them visually, as shown
above. The software should
snap them into place. Use the
Navigator area to zoom into the
preview and manually adjust
the image position as necessary.

3 *Photomerge* will start to
assemble the images
and will eventually open a
dialog window where you
will see the images stitched
together in a preview panel.
Any images that the software
cannot handle automatically
will be displayed above the
preview in a separate panel.

5 In the *Composition Settings*
area, click the *Advanced
Blending* check-box so the
software will do the best job
possible of correcting any
discrepancies between the
images. Click the *Preview*
button to see the result,
and when ready, click *OK*
to make the panorama.

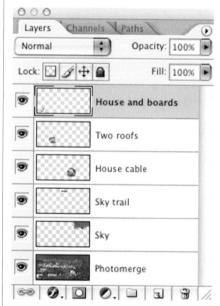

6 Now carefully examine the image for any problems caused by the stitching process. It is very rare for the image to be perfect at this stage. In this image we can see there are several alignment problems and a tonal problem with the sky in the top-right corner, producing a pronounced join (this is where the image was added manually in Step 4).

7 A quick and easy way to correct alignment problems is to open the original image that contains the affected part of the scene and make a random selection around the required area using the *Lasso* tool. Copy this selection from the original image and paste it into a new layer in the panorama, then move it into position over the fault. You may also need to use the *Transform > **Rotate*** or ***Distort*** commands to align the copy accurately. If necessary, add a layer mask to the copy layer and, with a soft, black brush, paint over any edge problems.

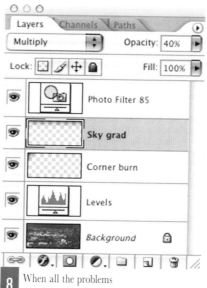

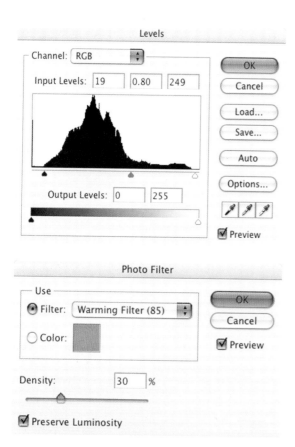

8 When all the problems have been dealt with, flatten all the layers, and use the *Crop* tool to finalize the shape of the image and remove the untidy edges left by the stitching. Now we can apply final contrast and color enhancements using adjustment layers. For this image I have increased the overall contrast, darkened the top-left corner, added a gradient over the sky to tone it down and, finally, added a *Warming Filter (85)* adjustment layer to lend a warm tone.

Tip

The process of creating a panorama begins with your camera and a suitable scene. Take several pictures of the chosen scene, starting at the left end of the view, and move the camera to the right between exposures. The number of separate pictures you need will depend on the angle of view you want to record, the focal length of the lens being used and whether the images are portrait- or landscape-oriented. The secret is to make each new image of the scene contain a good portion—30% to 50%—of the scene from the previous image. This gives the stitching software plenty of detail to work with.

PAINTERLY EFFECT

Photography and traditional arts have grown closer as a result of the digital revolution. As artists specializing in photography, painting, drawing, or other media have delved into the fascinating world of Photoshop to enhance their work, the boundaries have started to evaporate.

Although photographers have always had choices regarding the final media used for their work—for example in hand-coloring photographic prints with paints or dyes, or printing onto canvas—it is only by using Photoshop's artistic facilities that true artistic freedom is being experienced by many people.

This project can only scratch the surface of the almost limitless possibilities open to you, but one of the more popular techniques that people seek to replicate is that of giving a traditional, oil-on-canvas look to their work. This is the technique shown here.

1 Pictures containing bold color and strong compositions lend themselves to the creation of a painterly style, as the *Artistic* filters provided in Photoshop often reduce details and blend colors. Thus it is important that your image can withstand such changes and still remain interesting. The image of sunflowers used for this project is an ideal candidate. As usual, start by cropping your image and adjusting contrast and color balance. Then change the background layer into a normal layer by double-clicking on the thumbnail, and rename it.

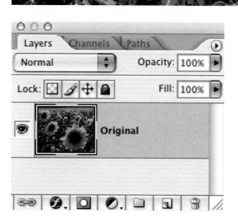

2 Make a copy of the image layer to preserve the original, and name it after the filter to be used. Here I named the layer "Dry brush." Now apply the *Artistic > **Dry Brush*** filter and adjust the settings in the dialog as desired, using the preview window to check the effect. If you prefer to preserve more detail in your image, use low settings in the filter dialog.

3 Now we can refine our image. To preserve the paint-effect layer we will use a new layer to create lighting effects. With the "Dry brush" layer active, press Ctrl (Cmd) + Shift + N on your keyboard to open the *New Layer* dialog.

Name the layer "Lighting", choose *Soft Light* from the *Mode* drop-down list, and click in the *Fill with Soft-Light-neutral color* check-box. We now have a new layer filled with 50% gray.

4 We'll add a little creative lighting to produce the chiaroscuro (the artistic term for light and shade) effect typical of old-master paintings. With the "Lighting" layer still active, open the *Filter* > *Render* > **Lighting Effects** dialog and either select one of the built-in effects from the *Style* list or define your own custom effect by dragging the handles on the light in the preview window. For this image, I chose the *2 O'clock Spotlight* style and slightly adjusted the shape of the light to make all four corners of the image darker. Also, the subtle colors applied to the light complement those of the picture, so adjust these according to your own taste and image. Adjust the *Opacity* setting to control the effect.

Tip

If you want to explore the possibilities offered by Photoshop's filters, open the *Filter* > **Filter Gallery** dialog, which allows you to access all the various filters in one place and preview their effect on your image.

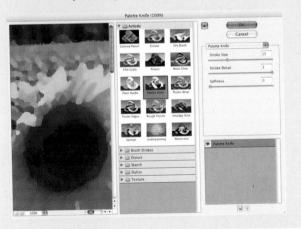

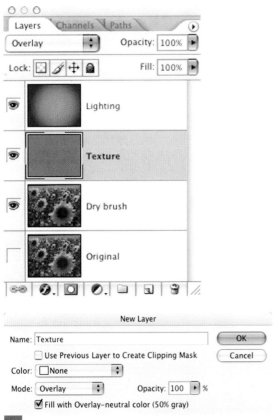

6 With the "Texture" layer active, apply the *Filter > Texture > **Texturizer*** filter using the settings shown to the right to create a canvas-effect surface texture. The lighting direction for the texture is set using the *Light* drop-down list, and for this image I set it to match the lighting direction on the actual subject. To make the texture effect more subtle, set the *Opacity* to around 40%.

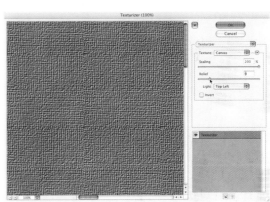

5 We can further add to the image by creating a canvas-texture effect on a new layer. Make the "Dry brush" layer active and press Ctrl (Cmd) + Shift + N as before to open the *New Layer* dialog. Name the layer "Texture," change the blending mode to *Overlay* and click in the *Fill with Overlay-neutral color* check-box. The layer will be created directly above the "Dry brush" layer and below the "Lighting" layer.

7 As a final step, you can make the texture effect sharper by applying some USM (*Filter > Sharpen > **Unsharp Mask***) to just the "Texture" layer, as shown here.

SIMULATING LARGE FORMAT

The ultimate tool for landscape photography has to be a large-format camera. The primary reason for this is that large-format cameras provide image management facilities not found on smaller formats. These image controls are known as camera movements.

Camera movements fall into two general groups: those that control image shape, and those that control image sharpness. Fortunately, using our image manipulation software, it is possible for small-format users to simulate some of the image controls. Image-shape control is used to produce what Ansel Adams called the "near-far" effect, which places more or less emphasis on a foreground object in relation to the background of the scene by changing the relative size of each element.

In this project we will use Photoshop's image-distortion tools to simulate the image-shape control available on a large-format camera.

1 In this simple scene I wanted to show the similarity of shape between the rock and the island in the lake. Although a wide lens has allowed me to emphasize the foreground rock, the island still looms too large in this image, resulting in the two main objects competing for attention. In such a case we need to reduce the size of the faraway element.

2 Using the *Transform > Distort* tools can result in lost image details at the edges, so it may be necessary to increase the canvas size to allow room for any changes in size. (In this instance it is not necessary.) For full control of the simulated large-format effect, the *Transform > Distort* tool is recommended since it allows linear stretching of the image. Here we see the use of the *Distort* tool to change the shape of the image, reducing the size of the background element but also elongating the main rock by dragging the bottom handle downwards.

4 Here we see the result of extensive retouching using the *Clone Stamp* tool. Compare the shapes and sizes of the rock and island in this image with the original, and note how the image now has more movement and energy.

3 Unfortunately, the *Transform > Distort* and ***Perspective*** tools leave behind blank image areas, shown above as gray areas, that need to be filled (although if the image has plenty of spare space you may be able to simply crop the image). Here I have copied parts of the shoreline rocks onto a new layer and positioned them over the blank areas. The *Clone Stamp* tool is used to make these new details blend into the existing image. Use the *Clone* tool to randomize the details to avoid repetition of shapes. The same methods will also be needed to create new lake and sky areas.

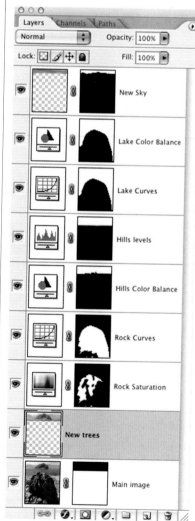

5 Use various selections and masked adjustment layers for localized tone and color enhancements. Here I have also altered the shape of the island in the distance using the *Transform > Skew* tool, as I didn't like the way it appeared to be leaning to the right. I have added a new sky to replace the original bland one, adding some much needed color. The final *Layers* palette is also shown for reference.

GLOSSARY

Adjustment layer Adjustment layers give you the ability to make non-destructive tonal or color adjustments to underlying image layers. The majority of the usual command-based adjustments are available as adjustment layers, such as Levels, Curves, Hue, and Saturation. The advantages of adjustment layers are twofold. First, you can make adjustment to an image without permanently affecting the layers below, and further adjustments can be made at any point during the image-editing process by simply double-clicking the adjustment layer in the Layers palette.

Alpha channel An Alpha channel is a special channel in addition to the standard Red, Green, and Blue channels, which stores information relating to pixel transparency. When you save a selection, or add a layer mask, you'll see an Alpha channel in the Channels palette relating to this saved selection or mask.

Blending modes Blending modes allow you to blend individual layers with the layers below. You select a particular blending mode in the Layers palette. By default, a new layer is always set to Normal mode, where the pixels on the layer have no interaction with those on the layer below. The actual science of blending modes is very complicated indeed, and by far the best method of using blending modes is by trial and error. By experimenting with different blending modes you can often create some very successful and unexpected effects.

Clouds filter The Clouds filter creates a cloud-like fill using random degrees of mix between the current Foreground and Background colors. The filter itself can be used for many effects, the least of these being actually adding clouds to a landscape! The effect of the filter can be softened even more, and made more subtle by blurring the fill after using the filter.

Canvas Size The Canvas Size command adds your chosen amount of extra space around the outside of an image. By default, the size of the available canvas is limited to the actual outer boundaries of the original image. You can choose how much extra canvas to add, and where around the image to add it in the Canvas Size dialog.

Channels A standard RGB image contains three separate color channels, specifically a Red, Green, and Blue channel. Each of these channels is a monochrome representation of which areas in the image contain more or less of that particular channel color. Channels can be treated in much the same way as layers, in the respect that you can make all manner of adjustments to each individual channel. You can even duplicate one or more channels and even merge them together.

Via the Channel Mixer command (Image > Adjustments > Channel Mixer) you can control what proportions of each channel are used to make up the combined RGB image.

Contiguous Contiguous is an option available with the Magic Wand tool. This indicates that any similarly colored pixels must be touching each other or interconnected before they are selected together with the tool. Unchecking this option indicates that similarly colored pixels should be selected together regardless of whether they are interconnected or not.

Dodge tool A tool that harks back to the days of traditional darkroom techniques, which can be used to selectively lighten the tones in a particular area of an image. The effect of the tool itself can be limited to the shadows, midtones, or highlights of an image via the Range option. The strength of the tool is controlled via the Exposure slider.

Desaturate A method of reducing the amount of visible color and decreasing the amount of gray in an image. The command Image > Adjustment > Desaturate completely removes any visible color, whilst desaturating via Image > Adjustment > Hue/Saturation allows the amount of visible color to be partially reduced.

Extract A tool or command accessible via Filter > Extract that allows you to extract a particular area of an image layer, designated by outlining and filling the appropriate area within the Extract dialog, and that renders the unwanted areas of the layer transparent.

Eyedropper A tool used to sample colors from an image or from anywhere on the desktop. The sampled color will be used as the current Foreground color. The tool itself can sample the color of a single pixel, or the average color within a predetermined group of neighboring pixels.

Expand Found via Select > Modify > Expand, this command will expand the outer edge of the current selection by 1 to 100 pixels.

Feather A command that softens the edges of a selection by a selectable number of pixels. The pixels around the edge, within the given pixel radius, are made progressively softer towards the outer edge of the selection.

Filters Automated effects available via the Filter menu in Photoshop, which can be used to apply a vast range of preset automated effects ranging from artistic natural-media effects to distortion, brush stroke, and texture variants. Most filters use a self-contained dialog box from which the variables within the filter can be controlled.

The effect on the image can generally be previewed from within the filter dialog before the effect is actually applied to the image.

Flatten The Flatten command, available via Layer > Flatten Image, collapses all visible layers into a single Background layer, enabling the saving of the file to a file type that does not support images containing separate layers, such as JPEG. Once a file has been flattened, the individual layers are no longer accessible, so it's best practice to save a version of the file first with layers intact as a native PSD file type, and then saving the flattened image under another name.

Fuzziness The Fuzziness slider, available in the Select > Color Range dialog, controls the degree to which colors matching the current Foreground color are selected by the Color Range selector. A high Fuzziness value will select all colors within an image that are similar to the current color, a very low value will select just those pixels that are a near exact match to it.

Gamma Gamma describes the brightness of the midtone of a grayscale tonal range. In a tonal adjustment command, such as Curves, the midtone point below the histogram is more accurately described as the Gamma slider.

Gaussian blur One of the collection of Blur filters that can be found via Filters > Blur, also one of the most commonly used Blur filters for accurate and infinitely adjustable blurring on an image or layer. The filter blurs an image by applying low frequency detail to it.

Grayscale What we generally think of as the black-and-white display within Photoshop. In this mode, an image can contain a maximum of 256 shades of gray. You can convert a color image to grayscale via Image > Mode > Grayscale. When an image is converted to grayscale, all color information is discarded.

Halftones Halftone images are made up from a pattern of dots, rather than continuous tones of gray, and are commonly used by Laser and Offset printers. The density of the dots within a haltone print give the impression of various shades of gray, a lighter density of dots appearing as a very pale gray, and dots packed tightly together appearing as near-black tones.

High key A high-key image is one where the majority of image detail is concentrated in the midtone to highlight areas. High-key images are very soft and flattering in terms of portraiture. A high-key image is easily identified via the histogram, where the majority of pixels will be concentrated towards the right-hand end of the graph.

Histogram A map of the distribution of pixels throughout the 256 levels of brightness within a digital image. The intensity of each level is represented across the graph itself from the darkest at the left to the lightest at the right. The amount of pixels at any particular value is shown by the vertical axis of the graph at that particular point. The graph itself can indicate, among other things, whether or not the highlights or shadows in the image are clipped, and this can be corrected by sliding the respective highlight and shadow sliders to the start of the histogram at each of these extremes.

Hue A value that determines the actual color we perceive. In essence, the value that makes Red appear as red, and Blue appear as blue. Where two colors are mixed, the hue changes accordingly. The actual hue of a color within an image can be adjusted via the Hue and Saturation command within Photoshop.

Inverse An option available via Select > Inverse, where the current selection is literally reversed, and unselected areas become selected and vice versa.

Invert Available via Image > Adjustments > Invert, this command inverts all of the colors and tones within an image, resulting in what we perceive as a negative image in regard to film photography.

JPG Compression A type of file compression used in the JPG file format that reduces the size or weight of the actual file by discarding image data, but maintaining visual quality. Although this form of compression reduces file size very efficiently, it needs to be used with caution, as using too high a compression level, or re-saving a JPG image many times can result in permanently damaged images. Overuse of JPG compression can also result in ugly JPG artifacts visible in the saved image.

Lasso A lasso designates a selected area within an image, enabling changes to be made to this selected area only. The lasso itself is shown by a dotted line, otherwise known as "marching ants." Typically, you would use the Lasso tool to generate this type of selection.

Layers Layers are at the heart of Photoshop image-manipulation, and can be thought of as separate sheets of acetate or duplicate images stacked on top of the original Background layer. By using layers, you can manipulate or paint onto an image without actually affecting a single pixel on the underlying layers. When you copy and paste parts of an image, the pasted image data is contained on a new, separate floating layer. Individual layers can be moved within the layer stack in the Layers palette, where the topmost layer will always appear to be in front of any underlying layers. When a new layer is added, it is completely blank until image

data is added to it. Any parts of a layer that contain no image data remain completely transparent.

Lens flare The Lens Flare filter, accessible via Filter > Render > Lens Flare, mimics the effect of a light shining directly into a camera lens. Within the Lens Flare dialog, you can control the position and intensity of the flare itself, and even reproduce the effect of a flare though lenses of various focal lengths.

Noise Noise can be thought of as digital grit or grain within an image, and can be used in many forms. The Add Noise filter, available under the Filters menu, can be used to add general noise to an image.

Opacity Opacity refers to the extent to which an upper layer obscures the contents of the layer below it. The opacity of the pixels on a layer can be increased or reduced in the Layers palette. By default, a layer's pixel content has 100% Opacity, so that any pixels on this layer completely hide the pixels on the layer beneath it, not withstanding the effects of any applied layer Blending Modes. The opacity of some of Photoshop's tools can also be modified, such as the Brush Tool.

Paths Any shape drawn with the Pen tool. A path is made up of anchor points joined by either a straight or curved line segment. The curved point within a path consist of Bezier curves, which feature two direction handles which can be dragged to adjust the actual shape of the curve. A closed path (where both ends of the path are joined) can be converted to a selection. Open paths can be stroked with any of the Photoshop painting or drawing tools.

Pixel A pixel is the very stuff of digital imaging. Any digital Photoshop image, or digital camera image is made up of millions of pixels, each one carrying specific color and brightness information. Although each pixel is a square block of color, when enough pixels are grouped together at a suitable resolution, the human eye interprets the collection of individual pixels as an image.

Quick mask An easy and accurate way of creating masks or intricate selections. Quick Mask mode is activated by hitting Q on the keyboard, and the initial red quick mask can be painted on to the image using any of the Photoshop painting or fill tools. On exiting Quick Mask mode, an active selection is generated, reflecting the shape of the painted mask.

Resolution Describes the number of pixels within a digital image. More specifically, the number of pixels per linear inch of an image. As a general rule, for images destined for print, the resolution of the image needs to be at least 240 ppi (Pixels Per Inch).

RGB color mode The default color mode used within Photoshop. Each RGB image is made up of four Channels, the first three being the Red, Green, and Blue channels—represented by grayscale channels in the Channels palette, each of these describing the proportion of these colors in the image. The fourth Composite channel is used for displaying the combined RGB channels in color.

Saturation Saturation refers to the vividness of any particular color. Just as desaturation removes color, increasing the saturation value of a color makes it move vivid and increases the purity. You can increase the saturatation of colors within an image on a global scale by going to Image > Adjustments > Hue and Saturation and make adjustments to the Saturation slider. To make targeted saturation adjustments, use the Sponge tool.

Stroke Applying a color, pattern, or gradient to the border of a selection, a path, or a layer. These strokes can be applied with any of the painting tools, via the Edit > Stroke menu, or via Layer Styles. Stroking a path with a brush (by right-clicking the path and choosing Stroke) is a very effective way of creating sophisticated line work in an image.

Threshold A command ideally suited to converting images to high-contrast black and white. The Threshold command, available via Image > Adjustments > Threshold, can be used to modify the darkest and lightest areas of an image, and drastically simplify the image as a whole tonally.

Transparency Parts of a layer that contain no image data are considered by Photoshop to be completely transparent. Photoshop supports 256 levels of Transparency, ranging from a fully opaque color or layer through to completely transparent. Transparency is indicated in Photoshop by a chequerboard pattern, which can be seen around the layers content in the Layers palette, or when the Background layer contains no image data.

Unsharp mask (USM) One of the Sharpen filters within Photoshop and one of the most flexible and frequently used. The filter itself works by creating halos around the perceived edges in an image, giving the impression of increased sharpness. Although the filter is very effective, it must be used subtly to avoid these halos becoming too exaggerated and obvious.

White point The exact point within a histogram where the pixels that are pure white feature. Ideally, this point should be directly below the point in the histogram where the white pixels appear, disregarding any tails in the histogram itself.

INDEX

ONLINE RESOURCES

Note that website addresses can change, and sites can appear and disappear almost daily. Use a search engine to help you find new arrivals or check old addresses that have moved.

Adobe (Photoshop, Illustrator)
www.adobe.com

Agfa
www.agfa.com

Alien Skin (Photoshop Plug-ins)
www.alienskin.com

Apple Computer
www.apple.com

Corel (Paint Shop Pro, CorelDRAW, Painter)
www.corel.com

Digital camera information
www.dpreview.com

Epson
www.epson.com

Extensis (Suitcase)
www.extensis.com

Formac
www.formac.com

Fujifilm
www.fujifilm.com

Hasselblad
www.hasselblad.com

Hewlett-Packard
www.hp.com

Iomega
www.iomega.com

Kingston (memory)
www.kingston.com

Kodak
www.kodak.com

Konica Minolta
www.konicaminolta.com

LaCie
www.lacie.com

Lexmark
www.lexmark.com

Linotype
www.linotype.com

Macromedia (Flash, Freehand, Director)
www.macromedia.com

Microsoft
www.microsoft.com

Nikon
www.nikon.com

Olympus
www.olympusamerica.com

Paintshop Pro
www.jacs.com

Pantone
www.pantone.com

Philips
www.philips.com

Photographic information site
www.ephotozine.com

Photoshop tutorial sites
www.planetphotoshop.com
www.photoshoptoday.com

Polaroid
www.polaroid.com

Qimage Pro (batch printing and processing software)
www.ddisoftware.com/qimage/

Ricoh
www.ricoh-usa.com

Samsung
www.samsung.com

Sanyo
www.sanyo.com

Shutterfly (digital prints)
www.shutterfly.com

Sony
www.sony.com

Sun Microsystems
www.sun.com

Symantec
www.symantec.com

Wacom (graphics tablets)
www.wacom.com

ACKNOWLEDGMENTS

A book, such as the one you are reading now, is the culmination of
many months of work by a whole team of skilled individuals. Each
of the professionals involved in the birth and realization of a new
book contributes their unique talents to make the book a desirable
and useful object for you, the reader. Although most of these people
remain anonymous, often as much to me as to you, nevertheless they
deserve a heap of credit for bringing this book to life. It is here, in the
Acknowledgments, that I as author of the book (and the one whose
name appears on the jacket simply because there isn't room for all
the other names) have the opportunity to thank all of those other
professionals who have made this book possible. So, thanks to all of you
at Ilex Press—it has been a pleasure working with you on this project.
Thanks especially to my direct contacts, Ben, Tom, and Jonathan, and
also to Alan Buckingham (the guy who originally introduced me to Ilex).

It is also always important to thank the people who live and breathe a
book along with the author while it is being written. In my case that is my
partner Barbara—thanks for all the kicks up the backside when needed.

I always enjoy constructive feedback from the readers of my books,
and thus be reached directly at les.meehan@zone2tone.co.uk
or through my website www.zone2tone.co.uk.